IRAQ 2016 HUMAN RIGHTS REPORT

Note: This report was updated 3/29/17; see Appendix F: Errata for more information.

EXECUTIVE SUMMARY

Iraq is a constitutional parliamentary republic. The outcome of the 2014 parliamentary elections generally met international standards of free and fair elections and led to the peaceful transition of power from former prime minister Nuri al-Maliki to Prime Minister Haider al-Abadi.

Civilian authorities were not always able to maintain effective control of all security forces which include: the regular armed forces and domestic law enforcement bodies; the Popular Mobilization Forces (PMF), a state-sponsored umbrella military organization composed of nearly 60, predominantly Shia components , which report directly to the prime minister; and the Peshmerga--the Iraqi Kurdistan Regional Government's (KRG) principal military force. Prime ministerial decrees on February 22 and July 27, as well as a November 26 parliamentary vote, boycotted by most Sunnis, established prime ministerial authority over the PMF; however at year's end the command and control over the PMF remained inconsistent and ineffective.

Violence continued to divide the country, largely fueled by Da'esh's actions. Violence occurred throughout the year as government forces fought to liberate territory lost to Da'esh, principally in Arab Sunni and some other minority and mixed areas. Armed clashes between Da'esh and government forces caused civilian hardship. At year's end the number of internally displaced persons (IDPs) declined to 3.03 million from a peak of 3.4 million in March. The decrease in IDPs was primarily due to Iraqis returning to their homes after those areas were liberated from Da'esh. The country also accommodated approximately 225,000 Syrian refugees, mostly in the Iraqi Kurdistan Region (IKR). Although donor funding increased, the government's response fell short of rapidly rising humanitarian demands, and displaced populations became destitute, leading some citizens to seek refuge abroad.

Severe human rights problems were widespread. Sectarian hostility, widespread corruption, and lack of transparency at all levels of government and society weakened the government's authority and worsened effective human rights protections. Iraqi Security Forces (ISF), members of the Federal Police, and the

Peshmerga committed some human rights violations, and there continued to be reports of PMF killing, torturing, kidnapping, and extorting civilians. Nonetheless, the terrorist organization Da'esh committed the overwhelming majority of serious human rights abuses, including attacks against: civilians, (particularly Shia but also Sunnis who opposed Da'esh); members of other religious and ethnic minorities; women; and children. Observers also reported other significant human rights-related problems: harsh and life-threatening conditions in detention and prison facilities; arbitrary arrest and lengthy pretrial detention, sometimes incommunicado; denial of fair public trial; insufficient judicial institutional capacity; ineffective implementation of civil judicial procedures and remedies; arbitrary interference with privacy and homes; child soldiers; limits on freedom of expression, including press freedoms; violence against and harassment of journalists; undue censorship; social, religious, and political restrictions in academic and cultural matters; limits on freedoms of peaceful assembly and association; limits on religious freedom due to violence by extremist groups; restrictions on freedom of movement; refugee and IDP abuse; both forced IDP returns and preventing IDPs from returning home; discrimination against and societal abuse of women and ethnic, religious, and racial minorities, including exclusion from decision-making roles; trafficking in persons; societal discrimination and violence against lesbian, gay, bisexual, transgender, and intersex (LGBTI) persons; seizure of property without due process; and limitations on worker rights.

The government announced investigations into reports of PMF abuses, but results of the investigations or convictions were often not publicly available. Information about government investigations or prosecutions of abuses by officials and members of the security forces was also often not publicly available. The KRG High Committee to Evaluate and Respond to International Reports considered charges of Peshmerga abuse, largely against IDPs, and exculpated them in public reports and commentaries. Impunity effectively existed for government officials, security force personnel, including the Peshmerga, and militias.

Terrorists committed the majority of serious human rights abuses. Da'esh members committed acts of violence on a mass scale, including killings through the use of suicide bombings and improvised explosive devices (IEDs), executions including shootings and public beheadings, as well as use of chemical weapons. They also engaged in kidnapping, rape, enslavement, forced marriage, sexual violence, committing such acts against civilians from a wide variety of religious and ethnic backgrounds, including Shia, Sunni, Kurds, Christians, Yezidis, and members of other religious and ethnic groups. Reports of Da'esh perpetrating gender-based violence, recruiting child soldiers, trafficking in persons, and destroying civilian infrastructure and cultural heritage sites were credible and common. Secretary Kerry stated on March 17 that in his judgment, Da'esh was responsible for genocide against groups in areas under its control, including Yezidis, Christians, and Shia Muslims, and was also responsible for crimes against humanity and ethnic cleansing directed at these same groups and in some cases also against Sunni Muslims, Kurds, and other minorities.

The government investigated some of Da'esh's human rights abuses, and in some instances, results were publicly available. For example, on August 21, the Ministry of Justice announced the conviction, sentencing, and execution of 36 men convicted of involvement in the 2014 Camp Speicher massacre of hundreds of Shia Air Force recruits after trials international observers criticized as unfair.

Section 1. Respect for the Integrity of the Person, Including Freedom from:

a. Arbitrary Deprivation of Life and other Unlawful or Politically Motivated Killings

There were numerous reports that Da'esh and other terrorist groups, some government forces, and militias acting outside government orders, had committed arbitrary or unlawful killings (see section 1.g.). During the year the security situation remained unstable due to widespread fighting between the ISF and Da'esh, and, to a lesser extent, the Shia PMF and Da'esh. During the year the UN Assistance Mission in Iraq (UNAMI) recorded a total of 19,266 civilian casualties: 6,878 killed, and 12,388 wounded. These casualty figures do not include the civilian casualty figures for Anbar for the months of May, July, August, and December. The corresponding period in 2015 showed 7,515 killed and 14,855 wounded.

Some security forces were alleged to have committed extrajudicial killings, although the government's identification and prosecution of specific killers were rarely made public. Ministry of Interior personnel allegedly tortured detainees to death, according to reports from human rights organizations. For example, Amnesty International (AI) reported receiving information that men wearing military and federal police uniforms unlawfully killed men and boys in a village north of Fallujah in October and in some cases tortured them beforehand (see section 1.c.).

Although officially under the command and control of the prime minister, some Shia PMF operated independently and with limited government oversight or accountability. According to multiple nongovernmental organizations (NGOs), more than 643 men and boys were reported missing near Saqlawiyah following the June liberation of Fallujah after PMF units intercepted them at ad hoc security screening sites. All 643 reportedly remained missing.

During the year Iraq witnessed frequent unlawful killings by unidentified gunmen throughout the country. For example, on February 11, a Kurd and a Turkmen Shia in Salah al-Din Governorate were killed in the center of Tuz Khurmatu in separate attacks; on April 29, a Sunni man in his 70s was killed in the Ma'qal area of Basrah; and on May 17, a local council member was killed outside his home in al-Amal al-Sha'abi neighborhood, northwest Kirkuk.

Terrorist activities continued throughout the year, particularly with Da'esh's attacks on cities. Baghdad was most affected, and was the site of more than half of the total fatalities. UNAMI reported that Baghdad experienced attacks of IEDs on a nearly daily basis from January to October. Some attacks targeted government buildings or checkpoints staffed by security forces, while others targeted civilians. Da'esh reportedly carried out attacks against civilians in Baghdad's Shia-majority neighborhoods. The largest was on July 3, when a coordinated bomb attack in Baghdad's Shia district of Karrada resulted in 292 civilians killed and hundreds wounded.

During the year authorities discovered several mass graves. On August 30, the Associated Press reported that analysis of satellite imagery identified a possible mass grave site at Badoush Prison near Mosul, where more than 600 inmates died. Approximately 35 mass graves in Sinjar District were found. In May media outlets reported the discovery of a mass grave in western Mosul containing the remains of 80 Yezidis. A representative from the Yezidi Affairs Council in the IKR reported these individuals were likely victims of Da'esh, and the remains showed signs of brutal treatment in captivity.

UNAMI reported that IEDs, suicide vests, and vehicle-borne improvised explosive devices (VBIEDs) caused at least half of all verified casualties during the year. Media reported that Da'esh IEDs infested Ramadi, which was nearly destroyed during fighting, which began with air strikes in July 2015 and ended with the capture of the city on February 6. Many civilians could not return to their homes because of the destruction and the threat of IEDs. UNAMI reported that IEDs placed in homes in Ramadi killed at least nine people in April. Spillover across the porous border from the conflict in Syria continued to destabilize the security situation in the country. The government's lack of the border with Syria facilitated Da'esh's movement of fighters and materiel into the country.

Ethnic-based fighting escalated in ethnically mixed governorates after liberation operations. For example, according to a January 31 Human Rights Watch (HRW) report, following January 11 bombings claimed by Da'esh, members of Shia militias reportedly abducted and killed scores of Sunni residents in Muqdadiya, in Diyala Governorate, and demolished Sunni homes, stores, and mosques. None of those responsible within the Shia militias were brought to justice by year's end. Media also widely reported instances when, after Sunni tribes turned against Da'esh and allied with the ISF, Da'esh conducted mass executions of tribesmen.

There were significantly fewer reports of killings or other sectarian violence in the IKR than in the rest of the country. Minority groups reported threats and attacks targeting their communities in non-IKR areas that the KRG effectively controlled.

On May 3, the IKR press reported several killings for which the families of the deceased alleged KRG security forces were responsible. On August 13, Wedat Hussein Ali, a journalist working for ROJ News, was abducted and later found dead. Media reports indicated his injuries were consistent with torture and quoted Wedat's family as saying the KRG internal security service had previously questioned him about his ties to the Kurdistan Workers Party (PKK). The press reported that the KRG internal security service temporarily detained several other journalists.

There were no known developments in other cases of arbitrary or unlawful killings reported in 2015.

b. Disappearance

Da'esh orchestrated most abductions, which focused on members of various ethnic and religious communities. There was no comprehensive account publicly available on the extent of the problem of disappeared persons.

In areas it controlled, Da'esh engaged in frequent abductions of members of the security or police forces, ethnic and religious minorities, and other non-Sunni communities. According to the director general for Yezidis in the KRG Ministry of Endowments and Religious Affairs, more than 2,900 kidnapped Yezidi men, women, and children had been rescued from Da'esh captivity by year's end, while another 3,735 Yezidis, mainly women and children, were believed to remain in Da'esh captivity. According to officials from the Turkmen Women's Association, Da'esh militants have kidnapped 500 Turkmen Shia women and children from Tal Afar and Mosul since June 2014, all of whom remained in captivity at year's end.

There were a number of disappearances and kidnappings that appeared to have been politically motivated. For example, on December 27, the Interior Ministry reported that unidentified gunmen broke into the home of female journalist and political activist Afrah Shawqi al-Qaisi in Baghdad and abducted her. Al-Qaisi regularly criticized the rampant corruption in the country. Prime Minister al-Abadi ordered the security forces to investigate the kidnapping and to "exert the utmost effort" to save her. There were no further developments by year's end.

Some militias exploiting the security situation carried out kidnappings, either for personal gain or for sectarian reasons. On June 22, the council of al-Quarnah District raised concern about the rise of child abduction, demanding that the security forces take decisive actions against it.

In December 2015, unknown gunmen kidnapped 27 members of a Qatari hunting party in the Muthanna Desert. The kidnappers released one Qatari and one non-Qatari member of the hunting party. There were no further developments in the case, and the 25 other members of the hunting party remained missing at year's end.

There were no known developments in other cases of disappearances from prior years.

c. Torture and Other Cruel, Inhuman, or Degrading Treatment or Punishment

Although the constitution expressly prohibits torture in all its forms under all circumstances, including cruel, inhuman, or degrading treatment, government officials as well as local and international human rights organizations documented instances of government agents committing torture and other abuses. Police throughout the country continued to use abusive and coerced confessions as methods of investigation, and courts continued to accept forced confessions as evidence. Da'esh, however, committed the overwhelming majority of such abuses.

As in previous years, abuse and torture occurred during arrest, pretrial detention, and after conviction. Former prisoners, detainees, and human rights groups reported that methods of torture and abuse included: putting victims in stress positions, beating, including on the soles of feet with plastic and metal rods, suffocating, burning, removing fingernails, suspending from the ceiling, overextending spines, denying sufficient water and the use of sanitation facilities, sexual assault, denying medical treatment, and threatening to rape female relatives of detainees or kill family members. A number of inmates reported that prison guards mistreated their families during visits.

International human rights organizations documented credible cases of torture and abuse in facilities of the Ministry of Interior and to a lesser extent in detention facilities of the Ministries of Justice and Defense, as well as in facilities of the KRG. The Human Rights Ministry and the Iraqi High Commission for Human Rights (IHCHR) noted that torture cases were underreported because many detainees were afraid to file complaints. HRW reported that widespread torture and systematic abuses continued in detention facilities and reported several instances of torture and rape of detainees. For example, according to NGOs, the men who had been convicted after confessing to taking part in the 2014 Camp Speicher massacre showed signs of torture. The International Committee of the Red Cross (ICRC) reported police and investigators continued to rely heavily on the evidence of secret informants or coerced confessions. Following confession, the coercion generally ceased.

The IHCHR could not confirm allegations of torture and systematic abuses in prisons and detention centers in part because the ministry was disbanded and the commission's last meeting of the year was in May. In February the parliamentary Human Rights Committee confirmed one case of torture in a Ministry of the Interior detention center in Baghdad; it was the only case the committee reported.

Abusive interrogation under certain conditions reportedly occurred in some detention facilities of the KRG's internal security unit, the Asayish, and the intelligence services of the major political parties, the Kurdistan Democratic Party's (KDP) Parastin and the Patriotic Union of Kurdistan's (PUK) Zanyari. During monitoring visits to IKR prisons and places of detention between January 2015 and June 2016, UNAMI reported 70 detainees had raised allegations of torture or other ill treatment during the interrogation phase, or both.

Abuses by terrorist groups were widespread. For example, in March HRW reported Da'esh fighters beat a man in custody every day for 18 days to force him to confess to selling cigarettes. The report also said witnesses reported 15 female Da'esh guards biting a woman in public as punishment for not covering her face.

On September 13, Da'esh reportedly cut off the feet of seven civilians from Hawija southwest of Kirkuk for urging residents to take up arms and rise-up against the organization. Human rights and humanitarian groups reported numerous cases of rape, forced labor, forced marriage, forced religious conversion, material deprivation, and battery.

There were no known developments in cases of torture and abusive treatment or punishment first reported in 2015.

Prison and Detention Center Conditions

Conditions at some prison and detention facilities remained harsh and life threatening due to overcrowding, abuse, and torture. There were also cases of food shortages and inadequate access to sanitation facilities and medical care.

Both the government and the KRG operated secret detention facilities during the year, according to international observers and to the head of the KRG parliamentary Human Rights Committee. There was no information available to verify whether--or the extent to which--they remained in use. In May HRW reported that Da'esh had set-up at least three prisons where former prisoners reported regular floggings and torture.

The Ministry of Justice reported that there were no accommodations for disabled inmates and the previously announced initiative by the ministry to establish facilities for disabled detainees had not been implemented by year's end.

Physical Conditions: NGOs, such as AI, reported overcrowding in prisons was a serious problem as the number of detainees increased as a result of the capture of suspected Da'esh members. Detainee conditions and treatment of detainees were generally poor, according to UNAMI's 2016 report, with overcrowding becoming a growing problem in most facilities. NGO contacts reported that due to the closure of prisons after Da'esh's 2014 advances, some remaining prisons held more than twice their designed inmate capacity. Three of the 24 correctional facilities managed by the Iraqi Corrections Service (ICS)--the only government entity with legal authority to hold persons after conviction--were not operational due to the security situation.

Prisons also became overcrowded in the South due an increased incarceration rate of criminals involved in drugs and kidnapping, and the transfer of 1,000 prisoners from northern governorates to Basrah. For example, the sole prison in Muthanna

Governorate should hold no more than 50 prisoners in each cell; however, observers reported more than 100 persons in one cell. Basrah central prison, with capacity of 1,100, held more than 2,500 inmates, and Ma'aqal Prison, with a capacity of 250, held 500 prisoners. Overcrowding exacerbated corruption among some police officers and prison administrators in the South, who reportedly took bribes to reduce or drop charges, cut sentences, or release prisoners early.

Many inmates lacked adequate food, water, exercise facilities, vocational training, and family visitation. Access to medical care was inconsistent. Some detention facilities did not have an onsite pharmacy or infirmary, and authorities reported that existing pharmacies were undersupplied. Moreover, NGO contacts reported a significant shortage of social workers at prisons. Women's prisons often lacked adequate child-care facilities for inmates' children, whom the law permits to remain with their mothers until the age of four. Limited infrastructure or aging physical plants in some facilities worsened marginal sanitation, limited access to potable water, and led to preparation of poor-quality food.

Authorities separated detainees from convicts in most cases. Prisoners facing terrorism charges were isolated from the general population and were more likely to remain in Interior Ministry facilities in harsher conditions.

Although the government held most juvenile pretrial detainees and convicts in facilities operated by the Ministry of Labor and Social Affairs, international and local NGOs reported that authorities held some juveniles in Justice Ministry prisons, Interior Ministry police stations, and other Interior Ministry detention facilities. Due to a lack of facilities in Maysan Governorate, juvenile offenders and adults were jointly incarcerated.

On May 3, AI reported that Shia militia units were holding more than 1,000 detainees, including some as young as 15, without charge in "horrendous conditions at makeshift holding centers" in Anbar Governorate (see section 1.g.).

Da'esh reportedly continued to operate three facilities in areas under its control, including the Justice Ministry's Badoush Prison in Mosul, and two Interior Ministry prisons in Ninewa Governorate. The condition of individuals detained in these facilities was unknown.

Published in its January-June report, UNAMI found overcrowding driven by terrorism-related detentions, such as in the Anti -Terrorism Directorate facility in Erbil. According to UNAMI, the KRG's new detention facilities in major cities were well maintained, although conditions remained poor in many smaller detention centers operated by the KRG Ministry of Interior. In some KRG Asayish detention centers and police-run jails, KRG authorities occasionally held juveniles in the same cells as adults.

Administration: Although there were credible allegations of mistreatment in both central government and KRG facilities, especially in pretrial detention, there was no information indicating that authorities undertook credible investigations into the allegations, and no prosecutions resulted therefrom (see section 1.c.). According to the Iraqi Kurdistan Independent Human Rights Commission and IKR parliamentary Human Rights Committee, instances of torture have occurred in IKR prisons. UNAMI reported during monitoring visits to prisons and places of detention in the IKR that 70 detainees raised allegations of torture or other ill-treatment during their interrogation.

The Ministry of Justice reported that budgetary constraints had significantly reduced the number of its visits to prisons. There was no information available about censorship or action on the complaints.

Recordkeeping on prisoners and detainees was generally inadequate. The Ministry of Justice reported it employed new technology to keep track of prisoners and detainees. The fully digitalized ministry-wide tracking system keeps track of judicial records relating to detainees and decreased the likelihood of individuals being detained past their release date. Moreover, it reduced corruption opportunities as prison officials could no longer alter prisoners' records in exchange for bribes. Despite these attempts at modernization, however, officials at the Ministries of Interior, Justice, and Defense, and at the Counterterrorism Service, indicated each entity maintained its own records, although some facilities held individuals detained by several entities, making it difficult to account for a facility's total population. Additionally, human rights organizations reported that prison guards or arresting officers released detainees after the detainees paid a bribe, a practice that further contributed to inaccurate detainee recordkeeping.

International and local human rights groups reported that authorities in numerous cases denied family visits to detainees and convicts. In many cases guards allegedly demanded bribes when detainees asked to call their relatives or legal counsel.

Independent Monitoring: ICS prisons allowed regular visits by independent nongovernmental observers. The ICRC continued to have its customary access to

Justice, Interior, Defense, and Labor and Social Affairs Ministry prisons and detention facilities. Authorities also granted UNAMI access to Justice Ministry prison and detention facilities in Baghdad. There were reports of institutional interference in prison visits, and in some cases institutions required advance notification to wardens and prison officials of visits by outside monitors.

The KRG generally allowed international human rights NGOs and intergovernmental organizations to visit convicted prisoners and pretrial detainees but occasionally delayed or denied access to some individuals, usually in cases involving terrorism. The UNAMI Human Rights Office and ICRC continued to receive regular access to IKR prisons and detention facilities.

Improvements: The Ministry of Justice reported that during the year it had installed surveillance cameras in all federal prisons, providing real-time information to a centralized office responsible for monitoring prisons. The camera system was meant to act as a deterrent to would-be abusers by allowing the government to record possible abuses for later investigation.

d. Arbitrary Arrest or Detention

The constitution provides some basic legal safeguards against arbitrary arrest and detention. Emergency laws give security forces broad discretion over arrest and detention when the government has declared a national emergency, which authorities declared in Baghdad on April 30 after protesters breached the International Zone. During the year there continued to be many reports of arbitrary arrests and detentions.

The government made minimal progress by year's end in improving enforcement of the rights governing arrest and detentions, despite the encouragement of an executive order and a reform law. In federal prisons the government reported the installation and use of video cameras to deter and record abuse.

In 2014 the prime minister issued an executive order to enforce the existing rights of detainees--a principal concern of Sunnis. The executive order prohibits the arrest or remand of individuals except by an order issued by a competent judge or court or in the conditions warranted by the code of criminal procedures. The authority that enforced the arrest warrant or detention is required within 24 hours of the detention to register in the government's central electronic and manual registers the detainee's name, place of detention, reason for detention, and legal article. The Ministry of Justice is then responsible for updating and managing these registers. The order requires the Ministries of Defense and Interior and the National Security Service to establish guidelines and mechanisms for commanders to register detainees' details in this central register. The executive order also prohibits any entity, other than legally competent authorities, to detain any person.

On August 25, the Council of Representatives (COR) passed the amended amnesty law. The reformed law permits retrials for detainees convicted on the basis of forced confessions or from reliance on evidence provided by secret informants.

After bombings on April 4, security forces in the southern governorate of Dhi Qar arrested persons under the Antiterrorism Law. Local residents alleged that the ISF used the bombing as an excuse to arrest innocent Sunnis, IDPs, and civil activists. For example, security forces arrested Mufeed al-Shanoon and Sala'am Dlejan, civil activists in the reform protests from Nassiriyah. By the end of the year, of the original 31 arrested, authorities released 18 for lack of evidence.

In August the human rights staff of an international organization reported concerns about government security forces, the PMF, and Peshmerga detention and arrest of IDPs. With the cooperation of the Ministries of Interior and Justice, the international organization representative visited IDP detainees, but authorities prevented the representative from conducting confidential interviews. Numerous reports of arrests and temporary detention by government forces, the PMF, and Peshmerga of predominantly Sunni Arab IDPs continued throughout the year.

Prison authorities sometimes delayed the release of inmates who were exonerated or who had served their complete sentence unless the prison authorities received bribes. According to NGO contacts, inmates whom the judiciary ordered to be released continued to face delays from the Interior Ministry or other ministries to clear their record of other pending charges.

There were many reports of Shia PMF forces detaining Sunnis following the liberation of Da'esh-dominated areas. For example, reports persisted that up to 3,000 prisoners were illegally held by the hard-line militias, Asa'ib Ahl al-Haq and the terrorist Kata'ib Hizballah, advised by members of the Iranian Revolutionary Guards' Quds Force. The prisoners included Sunnis and others suspected of working with Da'esh, and were held in up to five makeshift jails, some for alleged crimes and some to exchange for ransoms that help fund militia activities.

According to the PMF spokesman, the Justice Ministry appointed a judge who was, at year's end, working his way through 300 reported cases of abuse by militia members ranging from alleged prisoner abuse to summary executions. According to the spokesman, only approximately one-quarter of those accused were "genuine" militia members, and the rest were part of volunteer groups receiving no pay, medical, or survivor benefits from the government.

According to local NGOs and the head of the IKR parliamentary Human Rights Committee, prisoners held in KRG-administered Asayish prisons sometimes remained in detention for more than six months without trial. IKR police and internal security service officers in the IKR arrested protesters and activists critical of the KRG, and detained them for several days, according to NGO contacts and local press reporting. For example, Iraqi Kurdistan authorities in the northern city of Sulaimaniyah arrested 13 teachers on December 1, ahead of a demonstration over unpaid public-sector salaries.

Prime Minister Abadi said in an interview that some fighters participating in the battle for Fallujah had committed "mistakes." A government spokesperson later announced the establishment of a human rights committee to investigate alleged abuses. As of year-end, there were no updates regarding the men and boys who were missing in Saqlawiyah or concerning the progress of the investigation.

Da'esh continued to seize persons in order to silence its critics in the areas it controlled. In October, Da'esh arrested five former imams in Mosul on charges of sedition, according to local media. During the first week of January, Da'esh abducted five male teachers from around Mosul city for refusing to propagate Da'esh doctrines.

Role of the Police and Security Apparatus

The ISF consists of security forces administratively organized within the Ministries of Interior and Defense, the PMF, and the Counterterrorism Service. Interior Ministry responsibilities include domestic law enforcement and maintenance of order relying on the Federal Police, Provincial Police, Facilities Protection Service, Civil Defense, and Department of Border Enforcement. Energy police, under the Ministry of Oil, are responsible for providing critical infrastructure protection. Conventional military forces under the Defense Ministry are responsible for the defense of the country, but working with elements of the Interior Ministry, they often also carry out counterterrorism and internal security operations. The Counterterrorism Service reports directly to the prime minister and oversees the Counterterrorism Command, an organization that includes the three brigades of special operations forces.

The November 26 PMF law, one and a half pages long, was the latest in a series of efforts to place the PMF, composed of nearly 60 militia groups, under the ISF umbrella but reporting to the prime minister in a similar fashion as the Counterterrorism Service. Details on implementation, mission, and force structure of the PMF were not finalized as of year's end.

The authorities reportedly initiated some investigations of security forces accused of committing human rights abuses. As in the previous year, the minister of defense publicly called for holding perpetrators of human rights abuses within the security forces accountable, but there was little information available on the outcome of any investigations or of official punishment for human rights violations. On June 4, the government announced an investigation into "transgressions against civilians" and the PMF's killing of IDPs who fled Fallujah during the more than month-long struggle for its liberation. Authorities did not make public any findings of investigations by year's end, except the PMF spokesman's reference to a judge "working his way through" 300 reported cases of PMF abuse of which, he said, approximately one-quarter pertained to genuine militia members, while the rest pertained to "wannabe groups" like the Sunni Knights of Ninewa.

There were reports of torture and abuse throughout the country in Interior and Defense Ministry facilities. According to international human rights organizations, abuse took place primarily during detainee interrogations while in pretrial detention. The Interior Ministry did not release the number of officers punished during the year, and there were no known court convictions for abuse.

An NGO in Muthanna Governorate reported that guards on occasion beat prisoners for talking to outsiders about poor conditions and mistreatment inside the prison. On September 10, local media reported that authorities arrested and charged five police officers in the Rania District of Sulaimaniyah Governorate with torturing a man in their custody.

Problems persisted, including corruption, within the country's provincial police forces. The army and federal police recruited and deployed soldiers and police officers on a nationwide basis. This practice led to complaints from local communities that members of the army and police were abusive because of ethno-sectarian differences.

Security forces made limited efforts to prevent or respond to societal violence. Although 16 family protection units, located in separate buildings at police stations around the country, operated under police authority to respond to claims of domestic violence made by women and children, they lacked sufficient capacity. The most recent report detailing the units' work dated from 2014.

The two main Kurdish political parties, the KDP and PUK, had their own security apparatuses. Under the federal constitution, the KRG has the right to maintain regional guard brigades, supported financially by the government but under the KRG's control. Accordingly, the KRG established a Ministry of Peshmerga Affairs. There are 14 infantry brigades and two support brigades under the authority of the Ministry of Peshmerga Affairs, but the PUK and KDP controlled tens of thousands of additional military personnel.

The KDP had its own internal security unit, the Asayish, and its own intelligence service, the Parastin. The PUK also maintained its own internal security unit, known also as the Asayish, and its own intelligence service, the Zanyari. While the PUK and KDP took some nominal steps to unify their internal and external security organizations, they remained separate, since political party leaders effectively controlled these organizations through party channels. The KRG Independent Human Rights Commission routinely notified the Kurdistan Ministry of Interior when it received credible reports of police human rights violations. Local NGOs reported a sense of impunity among KRG security force officials; local human rights monitors reported an allegation of rape and manslaughter by mid-ranking officers during the year.

KRG security services detained suspects in areas the regional government controlled. The poorly defined administrative boundaries between the IKR and the rest of the country resulted in continuing confusion about the jurisdiction of security forces and the courts. Da'esh's control of parts of these areas exacerbated this situation.

Arrest Procedures and Treatment of Detainees

The constitution prohibits "unlawful detention" and mandates that authorities submit preliminary documents to a competent judge within 24 hours of arrest, a period that may extend in most cases to a maximum of 72 hours. For offenses punishable by death, authorities may legally detain the defendant as long as necessary to complete the judicial process. According to local media and rights groups, authorities arrested suspects in security sweeps without a warrant, particularly under the antiterrorism law, and held some detainees for prolonged periods without charge.

The government arbitrarily detained individuals and often did not inform them promptly of the nature of the charges against them. The government periodically released detainees, usually after concluding that it lacked sufficient evidence for the courts to convict them. Many others remained in detention pending review of other outstanding charges. The law allows release on bond for criminal (but not security) detainees. Authorities rarely released detainees on bail. KRG internal security units held some suspects incommunicado without an arrest warrant and transported detainees to undisclosed detention facilities.

The law provides for judges to appoint paid counsel for the indigent. Attorneys appointed to represent detainees frequently complained that insufficient access to their clients hampered adequate attorney-client consultation. In many cases detainees were not able to meet their attorneys until their scheduled trial date. There were reports that defendants did not have access to legal representation during the investigation phase, appointed lawyers lacked sufficient time to prepare a defense, and courts failed to investigate claims of torture while in detention. The Human Rights Ministry, which was dissolved in August 2015, acknowledged the need for public defenders and judges far exceeded supply, resulting in delayed trials.

Arbitrary Arrest: Police and military personnel arrested and detained individuals without judicial approval, although there were no reliable statistics available regarding the number of such acts or length of detentions. Authorities often failed to notify family members of the arrest or location of detention, resulting in incommunicado detention.

Pretrial Detention: The Ministries of Justice, Defense, Interior, and Labor and Social Affairs are legally entitled to hold pretrial detainees.

Although there were no independently verified statistics concerning the number of pretrial detainees in government facilities, most individuals in Interior and Defense Ministry facilities were reportedly pretrial detainees. In February the Ministry of Justice stated there were approximately 30,000 detainees in the ministry's correction centers, including 200 foreign detainees. NGOs noted actual detainee figures could be as high as 50,000. As of October 5, there were an estimated 1,681 pretrial detainees, including 82 women, at various KRG facilities, according to the KRG Ministry of Labor and Social Affairs.

Lengthy detentions without due process and without judicial action were a systemic problem. The lack of judicial review resulted from several factors, including a large number of detainees, undocumented detentions, slow processing of criminal investigations, an insufficient number of judges and trained judicial personnel, authorities' inability or reluctance to utilize bail or other conditions of release, lack of information sharing, bribery, and corruption. Overcrowding of pretrial detainees remained a problem in many detention facilities. There were allegations of detention beyond judicial release dates as well as unlawful releases.

According to some observers, authorities held many detainees for months or years after initial arrest and detention, particularly those detained under the antiterrorism law. Authorities sometimes held detainees incommunicado, without access to defense counsel or without formal charge before a judge within the legally mandated period. Authorities at times detained spouses and other family members of fugitives, mostly Sunnis wanted on terrorism charges, as proxies to pressure the fugitives to surrender.

KRG authorities also reportedly held detainees for extensive periods in pretrial detention. According to local NGOs and the head of the Iraqi Kurdistan parliamentary Human Rights Committee, prisoners held in regional government-administered Asayish prisons sometimes remained in detention for more than six months without trial. According to IKR judicial officials, IKR law permits extension of pretrial detention of up to six month under court supervision.

Detainee's Ability to Challenge Lawfulness of Detention before a Court: The constitution grants detainees the right to a prompt judicial determination on the legality of their detention, and persons arrested or detained may obtain prompt release and compensation if found to have been unlawfully detained. In practice individuals faced lengthy detentions without possibility of prompt release, regardless of guilt. Despite the 2014 executive order and the August 25 reform law concerning rights of detainees, NGOs widely reported that detainees had limited ability to challenge the lawfulness of detention before a court and that a bribe was often necessary in order to gain release. The law does not allow for compensation if a person was found to have been unlawfully detained.

Amnesty: There were no amnesty cases outside of the routine, religious holiday amnesties for minor crimes.

e. Denial of Fair Public Trial

The constitution provides for an independent judiciary, although certain articles of law restricted judicial independence. The country's security situation and political history left the judiciary weak and dependent on other parts of the government. Additionally, in 2013 the Supreme Court overturned a court order mandating the separation of the Federal Supreme Court and the Higher Judicial Council, thus allowing one individual to head both the court, which rules on issues related to federalism and constitutionality, and the council, which manages and supervises the court system, including disciplinary matters. Local and international media claimed the decision was politically motivated and undermined judicial independence.

There were reports that corruption influenced authorities' willingness to respect court orders. For example, the Integrity Committee of the COR reported that Interior Ministry and Justice Ministry employees frequently demanded bribes from detainees to release them even after court orders for their release had been issued, or after their mandated jail term had expired.

Corruption or intimidation reportedly influenced some judges presiding over criminal cases at the trial level and on appeal to the Court of Cassation. The Commission of Integrity routinely investigated judges on corruption charges, but there were numerous reports that such investigations often were politically motivated.

Numerous threats and killings by sectarian, tribal, extremist, and criminal elements impaired judicial independence. Judges, lawyers, and their family members frequently faced death threats and attacks. Lawyers participated in protests demanding better protection from the government against threats and violence. Judges were also vulnerable to intimidation and violence. In January unidentified gunmen shot and killed an investigating magistrate in Diyala Governorate. In February the president of the Basrah Court of Appeal survived an assassination attempt near his house in Kut al-Hijjaj.

The Kurdistan Judicial Council is legally, financially, and administratively independent from the KRG Ministry of Justice, but the KRG Executive continued to influence politically sensitive cases.

Trial Procedures

The constitution provides all citizens the right to a fair trial--but not necessarily a public trial--and the right to be present at their trial, with the assistance of free interpretation through all appeals, if necessary. Observers, including some government officials, the United Nations, and NGOs reported that trial proceedings fell short of international standards. Although investigative, trial, and appellate judges generally sought to enforce the right to a fair trial, defendants' insufficient access to defense attorneys was a serious defect in proceedings. Many defendants met their lawyers for the first time during the initial hearing and had limited access to legal counsel during pretrial detention. Trials were public, except in some national security cases, but some faced undue delays.

Accused persons are innocent until proven guilty under the law, and detainees are required to be informed promptly and in detail of the charges against them, as well as the right to a privately retained or court-appointed counsel, at public expense if needed. Nonetheless, officials routinely failed to inform defendants promptly or in detail of charges against them. Judges assemble evidence and adjudicate guilt or innocence. Defendants and their attorneys have access to government-held evidence relevant to their cases before trial and have the right to confront witnesses against them and present witnesses and evidence. In many cases, according to AI, forced confessions served as the only source of evidence without the corroboration of forensic evidence or independent witness testimony. The law provides the right to appeal, although there is a statute of limitations for referral; the Court of Cassation reviews criminal cases on appeal.

KRG officials noted that prosecutors and defense attorneys frequently encountered obstacles in carrying out their work and that prisoners' trials were unnecessarily delayed for administrative reasons. According to the IKR's Independent Human Rights Commission, detainees have remained in KRG internal security service facilities for extended periods even after court orders for their release.

Political Prisoners and Detainees

The government did not consider any incarcerated persons to be political prisoners or detainees and stated that all individuals in prison had been either convicted or charged under criminal law or were detained and awaiting trial while under investigation.

It was difficult to assess claims that there were no political prisoners or detainees due to the lack of government transparency, prevalence of corruption in arrest procedures, slow case processing, and inaccessibility to detainees, especially those held in counterterrorism, intelligence, and military facilities. Political opponents of the government asserted the government imprisoned or sought to imprison persons for political activities or beliefs under the pretense of criminal charges ranging from corruption to terrorism and murder.

Niaz Aziz Saleh, who was convicted in 2012 of leaking KDP party information related to electoral fraud, remained in prison following the completion of his sentence in 2014, according to the chairman of the IKR Parliamentary Human Rights Committee.

Civil Judicial Procedures and Remedies

Individuals and organizations may seek civil remedies for, or cessation of, human rights violations. Administrative remedies also exist, although due to the overwhelming security focus of the executive branch, coupled with an understaffed judiciary dependent on the executive, the government did not effectively implement civil or administrative remedies for human rights violations. In 2014 in collaboration with the IHCHR, the Higher Judicial Council established special courts to investigate human rights violations and reports of abuse wherever there is a court of appeal. On February 3, IHCHR members stated they had referred approximately 4,000 cases of human rights violations from 2015; however, the prosecutor dismissed hundreds of cases for lack of evidence or failure to complete required documents. At year's end the courts had not issued any convictions for human rights violations.

KRG law provides for compensation to persons subject to unlawful arrest or detention. The KRG's Ministry of Martyrs and Anfal Affairs handles compensation for unlawful arrests or detentions, and its Human Rights Commission reported that while approximately 8,000 cases (including many historical cases) received approval for compensation, the government was not able to pay compensation due to budget constraints.

f. Arbitrary or Unlawful Interference with Privacy, Family, Home, or Correspondence

The constitution mandates that authorities may not enter or search homes except with a judicial order. The constitution also prohibits arbitrary interference with privacy, but security forces often entered homes without search warrants.

According to accounts by family members provided to the UN High Commissioner for Refugees' (UNHCR) Protection Cluster, some government forces and militia groups continued to force alleged Da'esh sympathizers out of their homes in Anbar, Diyala, Kirkuk, and Salah al-Din Governorates. For example, in late October local security forces in Kirkuk allegedly evicted hundreds of households perceived to be affiliated with Da'esh before destroying their homes, although public statements by local authorities denied government participation in the forced evictions. Similarly, the Protection Cluster reported that in Diyala Governorate, local authorities announced in October that more than 6,300 IDP families residing in and around the city of Khanaquin would be required to depart their homes and relocate to IDP camps, or return to their areas of origin. According to the Protection Cluster, the order was in reaction to security concerns regarding the displaced households' possible affiliation with Da'esh.

A November 16 HRW report, *Marked With An "X,"* alleged that KRG forces, mostly Peshmerga, destroyed buildings and homes and, in many cases entire villages, making them uninhabitable. On April 4, the KRG, having been given access to HRW's evidence and findings prior to the publication of its report, set up a committee to investigate the allegations of unlawful destruction of property and movement restrictions on IDPs in territory under KRG control. The committee proposed that the destruction might have resulted from Da'esh IEDs, was part of collateral damage from fighting or bombing, or was required by the de-mining process to ensure returning IDPs were not injured by IEDs and booby-traps left behind by withdrawing Da'esh.

According to a November 3 HRW report, fighters of Asa'ib Ahl al-Haq detained and beat shepherds, including a boy, from a village near Mosul on suspicion of Da'esh affiliation, then stole about 300 sheep--the village's entire flock.

During the year Da'esh fighters entered homes, destroyed or looted private property, and converted houses into operational bases. Media reported throughout the year that Da'esh opened markets called "Spoils of the Nazarenes" to sell electronics, furniture, and other items looted from Christian homes. In January Christian groups reported that Da'esh arranged a market where they sold 400 houses, 19 high-rise buildings, and 167 stores, warehouses, and shops in the Mosul area belonging to Christians. In September media reported that Da'esh terrorists destroyed more than 17,000 homes in Salah al-Din, according to Governor Ra'ed al-Jabouri. In September, Da'esh reportedly burned approximately 25 homes of ISF members and government employees around Hit, northwest of Ramadi.

g. Abuses in Internal Conflict

<u>Killings</u>: During the year UNAMI recorded a total of 19,266 civilian casualties: 6,878 killed and 12,388 wounded, although how many civilians were intentionally targeted was not indicated.

According to the United Nations and international human rights organizations, some Iran-backed Shia militias, nominally under government control, committed human rights violations. The groups participated in operations against Da'esh as part of the PMF and were implicated in several attacks on Sunni civilians, reportedly avenging Da'esh crimes against the Shia. A few Sunni tribal forces that had rallied to the government, especially in Anbar Governorate, were also implicated in revenge killing of Sunni civilians, some of whom may have simply coexisted with Da'esh during Da'esh's rule in the area. UNAMI and HRW reported that members of Shia militias allegedly had abducted and killed scores of Sunni residents in Muqdadiya, in Diyala Governorate, and demolished Sunni homes, stores, and seven mosques following January 11 bombings claimed by Da'esh. In early January armed groups targeted Sunni mosques in Babil Governorate. None of those responsible were brought to justice by year-end.

Da'esh was the major human rights violator in the country, responsible for deaths of many innocent civilians. The United Nations, international human rights groups, and media reported that Da'esh executed hundreds of noncombatants. These included not only civilians who did not flee their homes in advance of Da'esh advances but also those who attempted to flee Da'esh held territory, captured or surrendered soldiers, police officers, and others associated or who had been associated with the government. For example, ISF discovered in November several mass graves containing the bodies of at least 400 former local police officers near the village of Hammam al-Alil, 19 miles southeast of Mosul. They appeared to have been killed at the end of October while in Da'esh's custody.

Media widely reported instances when, after Sunni tribes turned against Da'esh and allied themselves with the ISF, Da'esh conducted mass executions of tribesmen. For example, HRW reported they interviewed 20 residents in May from villages in Makhmur District who had fled to an IDP camp. The villagers said that before government forces retook the area in March, Da'esh executed government security personnel, civilians attempting to flee, and suspected government informants, while many others went missing.

Da'esh also reportedly killed and abducted religious leaders who failed to support the terrorist group. In September, Da'esh reportedly shot and killed two imams in eastern Mosul for not complying with instructions to encourage young men to join Da'esh and fight against the ISF.

Throughout the year Da'esh detonated VBIEDs and suicide bombs in public markets, security checkpoints, and predominantly Shia neighborhoods. For example, on November 24, a suicide truck bomber killed at least 77 persons, largely Iranian Shia pilgrims, in the southern city of Hilla.

On April 26, Yezidi religious leaders in Lalish published an open letter to diplomats and human rights organizations reporting 410 Yezidi men had been missing for a year after Da'esh transported the men to a mosque in the Da'esh-controlled city of Tal Afar.

Abductions: Militias, illegal armed groups, Da'esh, and other unknown actors kidnapped many persons during the year. While in some cases individuals were kidnapped due to their ethnic or sectarian identity, other individuals were taken for financial motives. Da'esh reportedly detained children in schools, prisons, and airports, and separated girls from their families to sell them in Da'esh-controlled areas for sexual slavery. Da'esh also punished minors in areas under its control.

UNAMI reported that Da'esh held approximately 3,500 persons in slavery, predominantly women and children from the Yezidi community, as well as other ethnic and religious minorities from the Sinjar District of Ninewa Governorate. On June 25, according to UNAMI, Da'esh moved 42 Yezidi women to Mayadeen in the Deir ez-Zor Governorate in eastern Syria and sold them to Da'esh fighters for amounts ranging from approximately 500,000 dinars to 2.2 million dinars ($450 to $2,000) each.

Kidnappings also continued to be a common tactic in tribal conflicts. In January members of the al-Halaf tribe abducted a man from the Garamsha tribe after the establishment of a truce between the two tribes failed. A photo of the man, bound and beaten, went viral on social media; the photo caption described him as a "captive of the war between the two tribes."

Physical Abuse, Punishment, and Torture: Reports from international human rights groups alleged that government forces and Shia PMF abused prisoners and detainees, particularly Sunnis (see section 1.a.).

Da'esh reportedly used torture and other brutal tactics to abuse and punish individuals connected to the security services and government, as well as those they considered apostates, such as Yezidis, according to international human rights organizations. According to a January-June UNAMI report, thousands of women, particularly those from ethnic and religious communities that Da'esh considered *takfiri*, or not conforming to their doctrine of Islam, had been subjected to rape, sexual enslavement, murder, and other forms of physical and sexual violence.

Da'esh forces killed civilians who cooperated with the government and anyone who refused to recognize Da'esh and its caliphate, or tried to escape Da'esh-controlled territory. During the first week of January, Da'esh abducted five male teachers near Mosul for refusing to propagate Da'esh doctrines. In March media widely reported that Da'esh electrocuted 15 civilians charged with spying for the government in Baghdad.

Da'esh attempted to attack both ISF units and civilian-populated areas with chemical substances, including chlorine and sulfur mustard gas. They developed a small number of crude chemical weapons that had a negligible effect on the battlefield. On March 16 and May 2, respectively, Da'esh fired chemical weapons into the Salah al-Din villages of Taza and Basheer, injuring more than 400 civilians, primarily Turkmen Shia.

Child Soldiers: There were no reports that regular ISF units conscripted or recruited children to serve in the security services. Some NGOs and an IDP camp manager reported that, while there was no instruction for children to join fighting, children continued to be associated with the PMF and militias in conflict areas. In August, NGOs reported Sunni tribal militias recruiting teenagers aged 15-17 from the Debaga IDP camp. KRG and independent sources alleged the Yezidi Resistance Forces and Yezidi Women's Protection Units militias employed Yezidi minors in paramilitary roles in Sinjar. For example, an HRW December 22 report documented 29 cases in which two armed groups affiliated with the PKK recruited Kurdish and Yezidi children, and abducted or seriously abused children who tried to leave their forces.

Additionally, armed Shia groups, under the banner of the PMF, continued to give weapons training and military-style physical fitness conditioning to children under the age of 18 at summer training camps. The government and the statements of Shia religious leaders expressly forbid children under the age of 18 from serving in combat; there was evidence on social media, however, of children serving in combat positions. For example, the official "Ideological Guidance" page of the

PMF website lauded a 14-year-old volunteer from Basrah for fighting alongside his father in Fallujah. The head of the UN Children's Fund (UNICEF) Basrah office said, "children from poor neighborhoods in Basrah are leaving school to volunteer" with PMF groups. The head of a Basrah NGO visited PMF units in Salah al-Din, where she encountered teenage volunteers serving on the front lines. On April 20, the United Nations verified 12 reported cases of recruitment of children by militias affiliated with the PMF, all of whom had been killed in combat. According to the IHCHR, during the year authorities detained 857 juveniles, including 804 on charges of terrorism, murder, theft, and kidnapping. An international organization reported that an estimated 30 percent of juveniles in pretrial or post-trial detention were held on security-related charges.

According to UNAMI, Da'esh forcibly recruited children to serve as informants, checkpoint staff, and suicide bombers. In January international media cited KRG sources who said Da'esh abducted up to 400 Yezidi children and trained them for combat or as suicide bombers. In March, Da'esh moved approximately 25 children from an orphanage in Mosul to a training camp in Tal Afar. The boys, some as young as eight years, included Yezidis and Turkmen, and were reportedly trained on weapons use and other combat skills. On September 20, Da'esh released a video that showed children executing prisoners in Mosul.

According to UNICEF, Da'esh violations against children included killing and maiming, recruitment and use as soldiers or suicide bombers, sexual violence, attacks against schools or hospitals, denial of humanitarian access for children, and abduction. For example, on August 21, police in Kirkuk cut a suicide vest off a 15-year-old boy wearing it under a Lionel Messi football shirt before he could carry out a Da'esh plan to detonate the vest inside a Shia mosque.

See also the Department of State's annual *Trafficking in Persons Report* at www.state.gov/j/tip/rls/tiprpt/.

Other Conflict-related Abuse: Active areas of conflict continued to disrupt the lives of hundreds of thousands of persons throughout the country, particularly in Baghdad and the IKR, but also in Anbar, Ninewa, Salah al-Din, and Diyala Governorates.

On October 25, UNAMI warned that expulsions of relatives of suspected Da'esh members were becoming widespread without due process, and that "collective punishment" endangered civilian lives and undermined efforts at reconciliation. For example, media reported in August that police forced relatives of suspected

Da'esh members to leave 52 houses in Dhuluiya, in Salah al-Din Governorate. On September 9, international media reported that authorities expelled the families of more than 200 suspected Da'esh members from their homes in Hit, northwest of Ramadi.

The government, the PMF, and Da'esh all established roadblocks that impeded the flow of humanitarian assistance to communities in need. The KRG--specifically KDP-run checkpoints--also restricted the transport of food, medicines and medical supplies, and other goods into Sinjar and Rabia Districts. NGO and diplomatic contacts stated the measures appeared to be aimed at limiting the influence of the PKK and their local affiliates, but they claimed unpredictability and the extent of the restrictions limited IDP returns to these areas.

Reports of Da'esh's targeted destruction of civilian infrastructure were common, including attacks on roads, religious sites, and hospitals.

Da'esh continued to attack cultural and religious heritage sites in areas under its control. On January 21, UNESCO reported Da'esh had destroyed the Monastery of Saint Elijah, which was more than 1,400 years old and the oldest Christian monastery in Iraq. On April 25, Da'esh destroyed Mosul's Clock Tower Church.

UNAMI stated in an October report that Da'esh violations against Christians, Faili (Shia) Kurds, Kaka'i, Sabaean-Mandean, Shabaks, Shia Arabs, Turkmen, Yezidis and others appeared to be part of a policy to suppress, permanently expel, or destroy these communities.

Da'esh increasingly used civilians as human shields in combat and targeted civilian areas with mortars. In May police chief Lieutenant Colonel Aref al-Janabi told local media that Da'esh took civilians, mostly women, children and the elderly, hostage in Albu Hawi and Hasi villages. He added that Da'esh terrorists used scores of civilians as human shields when tribal fighters, together with security forces, launched an operation to retake the two besieged villages. In October UN human rights spokesperson Ravina Shamdasani reported Da'esh had forced "tens of thousands of people from their homes in sub-districts around Mosul, and had forcibly relocated civilians inside the city itself" to "use them as human shields."

Section 2. Respect for Civil Liberties, Including:

a. Freedom of Speech and Press

The constitution broadly provides for the right of free expression that does not violate public order and morality, express support for the banned Ba'ath party, or advocate altering the country's borders through violent means. The main limitation on individual and media exercise of these rights was self-censorship due to credible fear of reprisals by the government, political parties, ethnic and sectarian forces, terrorist and extremist groups, or criminal gangs.

Freedom of Speech and Expression: Despite the constitutional protection for freedom of expression, government and KRG oversight and censorship interfered with media operations, at times resulting in closures of media outlets, restrictions on reporting, and interference with internet service. Individuals were able to criticize the government publicly or privately, but not without fear of reprisal. On April 27, the Iraqi Communications and Media Commission closed the Baghdad offices of al-Jazeera. The station's Baghdad bureau chief reported the government closed the office because it did not approve of al- Jazeera's editorial policies. The bureau chief also said unidentified armed men repeatedly threatened the bureau and its employees.

In April the media provided live coverage of Baghdad demonstrations, including protesters' first breach of the International Zone. When a second breach occurred, local media were quiet, with no live coverage or commentary. According to directors of two satellite channels, they received calls from "officials" telling them that covering the protests exacerbated the situation and asked them to "tone it down."

Press and Media Freedoms: An active media expressed a variety of views largely reflecting the owners' political viewpoints. The media also self-censored to comply with government restrictions against violating public order and because of a fear of reprisal, particularly by nongovernmental forces, but also by political figures. Media outlets, unable to cover operating costs through advertising revenue, overwhelmingly relied upon political funding, which diminished their ability to report unbiased news. Political parties strongly influenced, or controlled outright, most of the several hundred daily and weekly print media publications, as well as dozens of radio and television stations.

On July 13, the parliament introduced legislation on freedom of expression and peaceful demonstrations. NGOs, such as the Iraqi Union for Freedom of Expression, voiced concern about the legislation, specifically, that the law called for a one-year minimum prison sentence for insulting a religious symbol or figure, and required 10 days' notice to the government to obtain a permit for a protest.

International and local organizations reported arrests and harassment of journalists as well as closure of media outlets covering politically sensitive topics, including poor security, corruption, and weak governmental capacity. The deterioration in the security situation exacerbated harassment of journalists. Government and KRG security authorities sometimes prevented journalists from reporting citing security pretexts.

Local and national media extensively covered recurring protests in the South; however, security forces did not always allow coverage. For example, on February 12, security forces prevented a reporter for al-Baghdadiya TV from passing the security cordon to cover a demonstration. They told the reporter their security procedures prevented it.

On April 9, security forces wearing civilian uniforms reportedly attacked a Kurdistan News Network (KNN) cameraman in an Erbil mosque while the KNN crew was covering a protest there. As the cameraman attempted to film the protest, one of the uniformed security force members placed a weapon against the cameraman's head to force him to stop.

In the IKR, government authorities continued to try, convict, and take legal action against journalists, despite a 2008 law that decriminalizes publication-related offenses. According to Kurdistan Journalist Syndicate officials, the 2008 law is the sole basis for prosecution of journalists for publication offense under the regional counterterrorism law, for public morality violations and other crimes.

While in December 2015 the KRG reopened Nalia Radio and Television (NRT) offices that it originally closed in October 2015, Gorran-affiliated KNN offices in Erbil and Dahuk Governorates remained closed because of KRG pressure.

<u>Violence and Harassment</u>: According to a report of the Committee to Protect Journalists, 10 journalists and media workers were killed during the year. Five Iraqi journalists were killed covering the war with Da'esh, four by unknown gunmen, and one in a bombing in Baghdad.

Reporting from Da'esh-controlled areas was increasingly difficult. Journalists covering armed clashes involving government, militia, and Da'esh forces faced serious threats to their safety, with several instances of journalists being killed or injured. Military officials, citing safety considerations, sometimes restricted access of journalists particularly to areas with active fighting, but primarily to outlets not affiliated with the ruling party.

Media workers often reported they were under pressure from persons and institutions, including politicians, government officials, security services, tribal elements, and business leaders, not to publish articles critical of them. Media workers reported accounts of government or partisan violence, intimidation, death threats, and harassment. Mohammed al-Jabari, a correspondent for al-Made Satellite TV in Basrah, said he received a threatening phone call from someone at the Basrah Intelligence Directorate. He said this person was upset because al-Jabari reportedly recorded him talking about the deteriorating security situation with other intelligence officers at the governorate building. Al-Jabari left Basrah because of the threat.

During his coverage of a local teachers' demonstration, one of the security officers guarding the Basrah governor's office verbally harassed and beat al-Sharqiya News Channel correspondent Mazin al-Tayyar when he asked why the demonstration coordinator and another protester were arrested.

In April according to the Journalistic Freedoms Observatory, Sarmad al-Qasim, the editorial manager of the Lex News agency, received death threats for his work reporting government corruption in Diyala Governorate.

Throughout the IKR there were numerous beatings, detentions, and death threats against media workers. In some cases the aggressors wore military or police uniforms. Many attacks targeted independent and former opposition media, mainly the independent NRT; Payama Television, affiliated with the Kurdistan Islamic Group; and the KNN Television, affiliated with the Gorran Party. According to HRW, Wedat Hussein Ali, a Kurdish journalist who security services had previously interrogated, was abducted and later found dead on August 13 (see section 1.a.).

Censorship or Content Restrictions: The law prohibits producing, importing, publishing, or possessing written material, drawings, photographs, or films that violate public integrity or decency. The penalties include fines and imprisonment. Fear of violent retaliation for publishing facts or opinions displeasing to political factions inhibited free expression. Public officials reportedly influenced content through rewarding positive reporting with bribes, providing money, land, access to venues, and other benefits to journalists, particularly to members of the pro-government Journalists' Syndicate. These restrictions extended to privately owned Iraqi television stations operating outside of the country.

In 2013 the Iraqi Kurdistan Parliament passed the Access to Information Law, to provide for access to information for journalists, media outlets, and ordinary citizens. As of September, however, the KRG had not made efforts to implement the law. Moreover, local government, political parties, and officials, regularly discriminated against some media outlets regarding access to information based on party affiliation. For example, in KDP stronghold areas Dahok and Erbil, KDP-affiliated outlets Rudaw and KTV had access to all KRG departments, while in the PUK and Gorran stronghold of Sulaimaniyah, PUK-affiliated outlets such as GK TV and Kurdsat TV received more access to government and party information than other outlets.

All books published in the country as well as imported books required the Ministry of Culture's approval and were therefore subject to censorship.

Libel/Slander Laws: The law prohibits defamation and provides penalties of up to one month in prison or a fine of 50,000 to 250,000 dinars ($45 to $225). Many in the media complained this provision prevented them from freely practicing their profession by creating a strong fear of prosecution, although widespread self-censorship impeded journalistic performance as well. Public officials occasionally resorted to libel charges under criminal and civil law, which in some cases resulted in punitive fines on individual media outlets and editors, often for publishing articles containing allegations of corruption. When cases went to court, the courts usually sided with the journalist, according to local media-freedom organizations.

Libel is a criminal offense under KRG law as well, and judges may issue arrest warrants for journalists on this basis.

Nongovernmental Impact: Journalists and family members were targets of terrorists, religious groups that rejected media independence, criminals, corrupt officials, and unknown persons or groups wishing to limit the flow of news. Journalists were harassed, kidnapped for ransom, or killed in deliberate attacks for reporting information critical of Da'esh.

In April an armed group threatened two civil activists in Amara after they criticized Ammar al-Hakim, Islamic Supreme Council of Iraq president and Iraqi National Alliance chairman, on their Facebook pages. Hasaneen al-Manshad and Ali al-Dilfi wrote on Facebook that the Islamic parties were not fulfilling the needs of Iraqis and had failed to manage the country, in addition to criticizing Hakim's speech. The two activists were at a friend's wedding on April 7 when armed men from the Jihad and Construction Movement forcibly entered and threatened to kill them. The armed men held them at gunpoint until guests negotiated their release in return for the activists' public apology to Hakim and deleting the offending Facebook posts.

Internet Freedom

There were overt government restrictions on access to the internet, and there were credible reports, but no official acknowledgement, that the government monitored e-mail and internet communications without appropriate legal authority. Despite restrictions, political figures and activists used the internet to criticize corrupt and ineffective politicians, mobilize protesters for demonstrations, and campaign for candidates through social media channels. According to the World Bank, approximately 17 percent of the population used the internet in 2015, compared with 5 percent in 2011.

The government acknowledged that it interfered with internet access in some areas of the country due to the deterioration in the security situation and Da'esh's disruptive use of social media platforms. Representatives from the State Company for Internet Services reported they had pursued internet gateway projects that would give them greater control over incoming internet feeds as well as the ability to restrict internet content, but these projects had stalled. During the year there were reports that government officials attempted to have pages critical of the government removed from Facebook and Twitter for communications that the government considered "hate speech," although they did not succeed in doing so.

There were no reports the Ministry of Communications imposed social media blackouts. Sporadically throughout the year, the government shut down the internet during school exams, reportedly so students could not cheat. Additionally, at times the government shut down the internet during protests for a few hours.

Da'esh also restricted access to the internet and telephone service in areas under its control.

Academic Freedom and Cultural Events

Social, religious, and political pressures significantly restricted the exercise of freedom of choice in academic and cultural matters. In all regions, various groups reportedly sought to control the pursuit of formal education and granting of academic positions. The country's universities did not pursue gender-segregation policies. Da'esh continued to limit female education beyond the primary level in areas that it controlled.

Academic freedoms remained restricted in areas of active conflict and in Da'esh-controlled territory. Following Da'esh's 2014 seizure of Mosul, the group began reshaping education at the elementary, high school, and university levels, including printing textbooks for elementary school children that glorify violence and Da'esh history. For example, local and international media reported that at Mosul University, Da'esh altered the programs of study to comply with Da'esh ideology in the colleges of law, fine arts, physical education, languages, social sciences, and archeology. Da'esh extremists also targeted libraries, museums, and academic institutions in violent attacks and abducted students and faculty.

Extremists and armed groups limited cultural expression by targeting artists, poets, writers, and musicians. For example, Iraqi media continued to report that Da'esh had issued a directive banning all stores in Mosul from selling movies or music CDs, and had instructed businesses to stock only CDs containing Quranic verses or religious programs. On February 16, Da'esh publicly beheaded 15-year-old Ayham Hussein of Mosul for listening to western music, according to an HRW report.

In the IKR, according to local NGOs, senior professorships continued to be easier to obtain for those with links to the traditional KDP and PUK ruling parties.

b. Freedom of Peaceful Assembly and Association

Freedom of Assembly

The constitution provides for freedom of assembly and peaceful demonstration "regulated by law." Regulations require protest organizers to seek permission seven days in advance of a demonstration and submit detailed information about the applicants, the reason for the protest, and participants. The regulations prohibit all "slogans, signs, printed materials, or drawings" involving "sectarianism, racism, or segregation" of citizens. The regulations also prohibit anything that would violate the constitution or law; encourage violence, hatred, or killing; or prove insulting to Islam, "honor, morals, religion, holy groups, or Iraqi entities in general." Provincial councils traditionally maintained authority to issue permits. Authorities generally issued permits in accordance with the regulations.

In April and May, thousands of protesters took to the streets in response to cleric Moqtada al-Sadr's call for protests of the government's failure to combat corruption and provide security. Protesters stormed the International Zone in Baghdad and overran the Council of Ministers' Secretariat and the COR buildings, before ISF stopped them. Media reported security forces killed four and injured dozens of demonstrators with tear gas, water cannons, and live fire.

Most protests in the South during the year were accompanied by a heavy security presence and were peaceful. One notable exception was in Nassiriyah on February 2, when a demonstration turned violent after protesters reached the Da'wa Party's main office. They chanted that Prime Minister Abadi and former prime minister Maliki were "thieves," "Iran's spies," and "corrupt." Masked men with sticks came out of the office and began to beat the protesters. The police were present but did not intervene to stop the violence. The Dhi Qar Provincial Council formed an investigatory committee but did not identify any of the masked men or hold anyone responsible.

In some cases the government dismissed unauthorized protests or restricted protests for security reasons.

There were limited reports of violence or official interference in protests in the IKR. Media reported that on December 1, PUK authorities in the city of Sulaimaniyah arrested at least 13 teachers before a demonstration over unpaid public-sector salaries.

Freedom of Association

The constitution provides for the right to form and join associations and political parties, with some exceptions. The government generally respected this right, except for the legal prohibitions on groups expressing support for the Ba'ath Party or Zionist principles. The law stipulates that any person who promotes Zionist principles, associates with Zionist organizations, assists such organizations through giving material or moral support, or works in any way towards the realization of Zionist objectives, is subject to punishment by death. There were no applications of this law after the fall of the Saddam Hussein regime.

On July 30, parliament passed the Banning the Ba'ath, Entities and Racist Parties and *Takfiri* and Terrorist Activities Party Law, which observers portrayed as addressing the injustices of the de-Ba'athification process. Rather than ending the collective stigmatization of all those associated with the party, however loosely, the Banning of the Ba'ath Party Law arguably amplified rather than limited de-Ba'athification. Notably, while previous de-Ba'athification processes prevented individuals from political participation or certain economic benefits, this law criminalizes the very idea of "Ba'athism," metes out lengthy prison sentences for those promoting "Ba'athist ideas," and strikes at the heart of basic freedoms of expression, assembly, and protest, as well as the principle of nondiscrimination. The law specifically criminalizes "Ba'athists" participating "in any rallies, sit-ins, or demonstrations." Given the broad and wide-ranging definitions of Ba'athist activities and ideas, its stated application to "any entity, party, activity or approach," political parties, nongovernmental, civil society organizations and groups of citizens, demonstrating, protesting or simply holding meetings may violate the law.

Bureaucratic delays continued in the government's NGO registration process. The slow process impeded development and legal protection of NGOs. NGOs can only register in Baghdad, and must periodically reregister. The NGO Directorate in the Council of Ministers Secretariat issued registration certificates to 244 NGOs, from January to August. The NGO Directorate reported 2,844 registered NGOs.

c. Freedom of Religion

See the Department of State's *International Religious Freedom Report* at www.state.gov/religiousfreedomreport/.

d. Freedom of Movement, Internally Displaced Persons, Protection of Refugees, and Stateless Persons

The constitution provides for freedom of internal movement and foreign travel, but the government did not consistently respect these rights. IDPs had limited access to Baghdad, Kirkuk, and Najaf Governorates, and areas controlled by the KRG throughout the year. As of November approximately one million IDPs and 225,000 refugees were present in the IKR and areas under KRG security control. In late November hundreds of Sunni Turkmen IDPs from the Tal Afar area were denied entry into Dahuk, located in the IKR. The governor of Dahuk said he was concerned there were Da'esh elements among these IDPs, whose presence in the IDP camps in Dahuk among Yezidis might provoke revenge attacks on them.

The government generally cooperated with UNHCR, the International Organization for Migration (IOM),), and other humanitarian organizations to provide protection and assistance to IDPs, refugees, returning refugees, asylum seekers, stateless persons, or other vulnerable populations. The government did not have effective systems to assist all of these individuals, largely due to funding shortfalls, lack of capacity, and lack of access. The security situation and armed clashes between the ISF and Da'esh throughout the year caused significant movement of civilians, further complicating the government's coordination of relief efforts. The IOM estimated that, since the beginning of 2014, the conflict with Da'esh had caused more than 3.4 million individuals to become displaced, at least one million of whom have returned home. Security considerations in and near active combat areas, unexploded ordinance, destruction of infrastructure, and official and unofficial restrictions continued to limit humanitarian access to IDP communities.

Abuse of Migrants, Refugees, and Stateless Persons: UN agencies, NGOs and the press reported that sectarian groups, extremists, criminals, and, in some alleged but unverified cases, government forces attacked and arrested refugees, including Palestinians, Ahwazis, and Syrian Arabs.

Local NGOs reported that abuse of Syrian refugees--often by other refugees--was common, including violence against women and children, child marriage, forced prostitution, and sexual harassment.

A 2011 memorandum of understanding between the government and the United Nations provided for the closure of Camp Ashraf in Diyala Governorate, and transfer to Camp Hurriya (in Baghdad) of members of the Mujahedin-e-Khalq (MeK), an Iranian dissident group. The UNHCR relocation program provided the means successfully to relocate all MeK members from Iraq to third countries during the year; the majority of MeK were moved to Albania.

In-country Movement: The law permits security forces to restrict in-country movement pursuant to a warrant, impose a curfew, cordon off and search an area, and take other necessary security and military measures in response to security threats and attacks. There were numerous reports that security forces, including the ISF and Peshmerga, as well as the PMF, selectively enforced regulations requiring residency permits to limit entry of persons into liberated areas under their control. UNAMI and the UN Office of the High Commissioner for Human Rights received multiple reports that Kirkuk authorities denied Sunni Arab IDPs from Salah al-Din and Ninewa Governorates access to Kirkuk Governorate.

UNAMI reported that in some areas, civilians fleeing conflict zones were intercepted by armed groups and militia operating in support of the ISF, and were targeted for threats, intimidation, physical violence, abductions, destruction of property, and killings. There were a number of reports that IDPs faced hostility from local government authorities and populations, as well as threats of expulsion.

UNHCR reported that Kirkuk authorities also confiscated identification documents or served notices of eviction to IDPs from Salah al-Din, Anbar, and Diyala Governorates, provoking their departure from camps and urban centers. On September 22, authorities forcibly returned 330 IDP families from Laylan Camp to a checkpoint along the road to Salah al-Din, according to the Iraq Humanitarian Protection Cluster. From September 1 to 21, Protection Cluster partners documented the departure of more than 1,000 IDP families who had been targeted for expulsion by local authorities. Amnesty International reported that the PMF Units (predominantly Shi'a militias) and the Peshmerga forces prevented civilians, largely Sunni, from returning to their homes after Da'esh was pushed out.

The KRG, imposing what it stated were necessary security procedures, restricted movement across the areas it administered. Authorities required nonresidents of the IKR to obtain permits that authorized limited stays in the IKR. These permits were generally renewable. Iraqi citizens from outside the IKR who sought to obtain residency permits for KRG-controlled areas required sponsorship from a resident in the region. Citizens (of all ethno-sectarian backgrounds, including Kurds) crossing into the region from the South were obligated to enter at checkpoints and undergo personal and vehicle inspection. The government imposed similar restrictions on IDPs from Ninewa Governorate and the disputed territories.

KRG authorities applied restrictions more stringently in some areas than in others. The United Nations and international humanitarian organizations alleged that practices regarding the entry of IDPs and Iraqi refugees seeking to return were more or less restrictive depending upon the location of the checkpoint and the ethno-sectarian background of the displaced individuals. There were also reports that checkpoints into the IKR were sometimes closed for extended periods, forcing IDPs to wait to enter the region. Officials prevented individuals whom they deemed security threats from entering the region. IKR officials generally admitted minority IDPs into the IKR, although the security checks were occasionally lengthy. Entry often was more difficult for men, particularly Arab men traveling without family.

Due to military operations aimed at defeating Da'esh, ISF, including the PMF and KRG Peshmerga, increased the number of checkpoints and erected makeshift roadblocks in many parts of the country (see section 1.g.). In June, following the liberation of Ramadi and Fallujah from Da'esh in Anbar Governorate, thousands of residents fled those cities for surrounding areas. Most were prevented from leaving Anbar per an official government order, due to security and ethnocentric concerns. Some 70,000 individuals fled Fallujah during a three-day period in June when the Iraqi army secured safe exit routes, overwhelming local and international assistance efforts and leaving many stranded in the desert for days without aid. At least 600 IDPs from Fallujah were missing after Shia PMF units held them for screening. IDPs began returning to Fallujah and outlying areas in September, although there were credible reports that provincial authorities required some government workers to return before they were ready to do so. In September, IDPs in Laylan Camp in Kirkuk were informed that they must return to their areas of origin. UN agencies confirmed that confiscation of identification documents and other measures to force IDPs to return home continued.

Da'esh restricted freedom of movement, particularly in the West and North (see section 1.g.). Da'esh prevented citizens from leaving the cities of Fallujah, Ramadi, Mosul, and other places unless those citizens paid bribes to exit, left family members behind as collateral for their return, or agreed to relinquish property they owned in those cities. Da'esh severely restricted women's freedom of movement in areas under its control. Patrols checked to make sure women wore suitable attire and that male relatives or guardians accompanied them outside the home. There were credible reports that Da'esh killed civilians trying to flee, including in the cities of Hawija, Qayara, and Mosul, when ISF moved to liberate those areas.

Foreign Travel: The government required exit permits for citizens leaving the country, but the requirement was not routinely enforced.

Exile: The constitution permits forced exile only of naturalized citizens and only if a judicial decision establishes that the individual obtained citizenship based on material falsifications. There were no reported cases of forced exile. After 2003 many former Ba'ath Party members sought refuge in neighboring countries, choosing self-imposed exile over possible prosecutions under de-Ba'athification laws, and later under the Anti-Terrorism Law. In 2011 another wave of prominent Sunni politicians left the country after the government began arresting Sunnis and dissidents, by expansively applying Anti-Terrorism Law provisions.

<u>Emigration and Repatriation</u>: The government failed to provide travel documents to hundreds of citizens awaiting deportation from the United States, essentially rendering these individuals stateless.

Internally Displaced Persons

The constitution and the national policy on displacement address IDP rights, but few laws specifically do so. The central government, the IKR, and international organizations, including UN agencies and NGOs, attempted to provide protection and other assistance to IDPs. Host communities were strained as the number of IDPs outside of camps increased. In 2014 the United Nations designated the humanitarian crisis as a Level Three emergency, its highest level, citing the scale, urgency, and complexity of the situation and has since extended the designation through February 2017.

Since 2014 the armed conflict has displaced more than 3.4 million persons, predominantly from Anbar, Ninewa, and Salah al-Din Governorates. In July and August, Salah al-Din Governorate experienced a significant increase in new IDPs resulting from the positioning of government forces in areas around Mosul in preparation for the operations for its liberation. From mid-June through mid-December, nearly 131,000 persons were displaced from Ninewa, Salah al-Din, and Erbil Governorates. One million IDPs from the 2006-08 sectarian conflict remained as of 2014, presumed to be included in the total IDP figure nationwide.

Sectarian violence and the advance of Da'esh displaced Sunni, Christian, Shia, Yezidi, Turkmen, Shabak, and Sabaean-Mandean families (see section 1.g.). While some of the displaced fled to areas outside their districts of origin, lack of secure corridors and fear of looting made others decide to stay. The government urged civilians in Mosul to remain in their homes, attempting to limit possible displacement during the Mosul operations.

The government's focus on military operations to expel Da'esh and address IDPs' immediate humanitarian needs, strained official efforts to promote safe, voluntary return or local integration. This challenge required the government to balance attempts to assist IDPs while maintaining good relations with host communities, including addressing their concerns about security threats posed by IDPs. UNHCR and other international organizations noted there was no national policy on IDP returns to homes of origin. In September the Ministry of Displacement and Migration and IKR's Ministry of Interior signed a Memorandum of Understanding to develop a coordinated approach on IDP returns and other IDP issues. The

Ministry of Displacement and Migration's strategy recognized local integration as a legal option for IDPs; although in practice, new IDPs arriving from Da'esh-controlled areas (the large majority of whom were Sunni Arabs) faced difficulties being accepted in KRG-controlled areas or in areas held by Shia PMF units. The government attempted to integrate IDPs into local populations but also encouraged families to return to their original homes, in some cases before the families were willing to return.

Government assistance focused on the provision of financial grants, but it made neither the initial nor the successive payments consistently, particularly with the downturn in the economy. Faced with the large movements of IDPs across the country, the government provided food, water, and financial assistance to many but not all IDPs, including in the IKR. Many IDPs lived in informal settlements where they did not receive adequate water, sanitation, or other essential services. According to the IOM, as of November, 17 percent of IDPs lived in shelter arrangements that did not meet minimal safety or security standards, and approximately 64 percent resided in private arrangements, including host family residences, hotels, motels, and rented housing. The government and KRG worked with the United Nations to expand existing camp infrastructure.

In June nearly 85,000 IDPs from Fallujah and surrounding areas fled military operations to expel Da'esh. The unexpectedly large number of IDPs fleeing in a short period of time initially overwhelmed assistance efforts. Since June military shaping operations in villages south of Mosul displaced nearly 131,000 civilians. Many of them fled to overcrowded IDP camps in Debaga and elsewhere. The government worked with UN agencies and NGOs to provide food, shelter, health care, water and sanitation, and other essential services to IDPs in camps and other informal settlements. The government provided many of the IDPs in the camps with basic household goods.

All citizens are eligible to receive food under the Public Distribution System (PDS); however, PDS was implemented sporadically and irregularly. Not all commodities were distributed each month and not all IDPs were able to access the PDS in each governorate. Since the price of oil has dropped, the functioning of the PDS has been even more irregular. Iraqis could only redeem their PDS rations at their place of residence and within their registered governorate, thus losing access and entitlement following displacement.

Persons who did not register as IDPs in their current places of residence sometimes faced limited access to services. Local authorities often determined whether IDPs would have access to local services. Through the provision of legal aid, UNHCR and other humanitarian actors assisted IDPs in obtaining documentation and registering with authorities to improve access to services and entitlements. The IOM reported that some IDPs faced difficulty with registration due to lack of required documentation and administrative delays.

While humanitarian assistance generally reached IDPs in most of the country, access to those remaining in Da'esh-controlled areas was limited. Humanitarian personnel continued to attempt to provide assistance in these areas, but security and movement limitations constrained aid delivery.

Protection of Refugees

Access to Asylum: The law provides for the granting of asylum or refugee status, and the government established a system, albeit flawed, for providing protection to refugees. According to UNHCR, there were approximately 267,000 refugees in the country, most of whom are asylum seekers arriving from Syria, with smaller numbers from Iran and Turkey. The government generally cooperated with UNHCR and other humanitarian organizations to provide protection and assistance to refugees and IDPs in the country.

Refoulement: The government cooperated with UNHCR to prevent the deportation of refugees. UNHCR relocated refugees at risk of deportation to refugee camps or attempted to resettle them.

Employment: Refugees and asylum seekers are legally entitled to work in the private sector. Palestinian refugees, however, faced job insecurity when working in the public sector due to their ambiguous legal status; the government did not recognize their refugee status and did not allow them to obtain citizenship. Syrian refugees were able to obtain and renew residency and work permits both in refugee camps and in Erbil. Authorities, however, did not allow some Syrian refugees to continue their employment in refugee camps.

Durable Solutions: Ethnic Kurdish refugees from Syria, Turkey, and Iran in the IKR generally integrated well, although economic hardship plagued families and prevented many children, especially Syrians, from enrolling in formal school. Local integration remained the best and most likely option for the majority of Iranian Kurds. In September the KRG reported that approximately 60 percent of Syrian refugees in the IKR lived outside camps. Many worked in Erbil or found shelter with relatives in the IKR.

Stateless Persons

UNHCR estimated that approximately 50,000 stateless persons lived in the country, many of them Syrian refugees. Many nonrefugee stateless individuals had previously been citizens and had already begun the process of reacquiring nationality.

As of 2006, the latest year for which data was available, an estimated 54,500 Bidoun individuals living as nomads in the desert near or in the southern governorates of Basrah, Dhi Qar, and Qadisiyah remained undocumented and stateless. Prolonged drought in the southern section of the country forced many individuals from these communities to migrate to city centers, where most obtained identification documents and gained access to food rations and other social benefits. Other communities similarly at risk of statelessness included the country's Romani population, the Ahwazi community of Shia Arabs of Iranian descent, the Bahai religious minority community, inhabitants of the southern Marshlands, members of the Goyan and Omariya Turkish Kurdish tribes near Mosul, and nationals of South Sudan, which had not established a diplomatic presence in the country.

Stateless persons faced discrimination in employment and access to education. Many stateless persons, particularly Baha'i, were not able to register for identity cards, which prevented them from enrolling in public school, registering marriages, and gaining access to some government services. Stateless persons also faced difficulty obtaining public-sector employment and lacked job security.

Section 3. Freedom to Participate in the Political Process

The constitution provides citizens the ability to choose their government in free and fair periodic elections held by secret ballot and based on universal and equal suffrage. Despite violence and other past irregularities in the conduct of elections, citizens generally exercised this right.

Elections and Political Participation

Recent Elections: In 2014 the Independent High Electoral Commission (IHEC) conducted elections for both the Iraqi Council of Representatives and the provincial councils of Erbil, Dahuk, and Sulaimaniyah Governorates. International and local observers monitored the elections. Despite security concerns, monitors declared the elections credible and free from widespread or systemic fraud. There were limited reports of abuse or electoral irregularities. IHEC announced preliminary election results, and the Federal Supreme Court certified the results in 2014.

The loss of civil documentation related to a growing number of IDPs presented a challenge for future elections. IHEC representatives visited an IDP camp in Basrah to renew the voter registrations of camp residents but could not do so because several persons were missing identification documentation. The same lack of identification documents applied to many IDPs across the country.

In 2015 the IKR established the Kurdistan Independent High Electoral Commission, which has authority to supervise all elections and referenda within the IKR, previously under IHEC supervision. There were no elections or referenda in the IKR during the year.

In 2015 IHEC announced initial approval for a petition by Basrah Governorate residents to hold a referendum to make the governorate an autonomous region. As of December the referendum was not yet held because of insufficient funds, as well as declining political support for the initiative.

Political Parties and Political Participation: Political parties and coalition blocs tended to organize along either religious or ethnic lines. Membership in some political parties conferred special privileges and advantages in employment and education.

The Iraqi Kurdistan Region Parliament (IKP) had not convened since October 2015, when KDP officials and politicians ordered their counterparts in Gorran Party, including IKP speaker Yousif Mohammed, to leave Erbil and not report to parliament. KRG security forces subsequently blocked Mohammed from returning to Erbil. Negotiations among IKR political parties to reactivate parliament continued sporadically throughout the year.

Participation of Women and Minorities: The constitution mandates that women must constitute at least 25 percent of parliamentary and provincial council membership. In the parliamentary elections, 22 women received sufficient votes to win seats in the 328-seat COR without having to rely on the constitutional quota, compared with five in 2010. More than 60 additional women were awarded seats based on the quota, bringing the total number of seats women held to 86. Despite an increase in the number of female parliamentarians, political discussions often marginalized female members of parliament. There was one woman in the Council of Ministers.

Of the 328 seats in parliament, the law reserves eight seats for minorities: five for Christian candidates from Baghdad, Ninewa, Kirkuk, Erbil, and Dahuk; one Yezidi; one Sabaean-Mandean; and one Shabak.

Section 4. Corruption and Lack of Transparency in Government

The law provides criminal penalties for corruption by officials, but the government did not implement the law effectively. There were numerous reports of government corruption during the year. Officials in all parts of the government often engaged in corrupt practices with impunity, and investigation of corruption was not free from political influence. Family, tribal, and religious considerations significantly influenced government decisions at all levels. Bribery, money laundering, nepotism, and misappropriation of public funds were common.

Corruption: On August 25, the COR used secret ballots to remove Defense Minister Khaled al-Obaidi from his office, and on September 21, it also removed Finance Minister Hoshyar Zebari. The questioning and subsequent no confidence votes were reportedly to root out corruption, but media reported that some thought it was to advance the politically motivated agenda of former prime minister Nuri al-Maliki.

The Commission of Integrity (COI) refrained from releasing the names of government officials in its semiannual report. In July the COI published a semiannual report covering activities from January to June. The commission investigated 13,226 cases of corruption, adjudicated 7,088 cases, and referred 1,891 cases to courts for trial. Six of the cases referred to the courts involved ministers, and 99 director general-level officials. The COI reportedly recovered 135.3 billion dinars ($130 million).

There were reports alleging that senior officials involved in bribery schemes held illicit funds in overseas accounts, making bribery more difficult to detect. In 2015 international media reported that the government launched a corruption investigation against the former deputy prime minister for energy affairs Baha al-Araji, accusing him of nine crimes, including property racketeering and financial corruption. Araji publicly acknowledged owning as many as seven houses, a hotel, and other properties. He also had 300 guards whose salaries were paid by the state. In February the COI announced Araji had been referred to the integrity court on charges of corruption, but at year's end, no charges or arrest warrants had been filed against him. In 2015 the judiciary announced it had issued an arrest warrant for Minister of Trade Milas Muhammad Abdul Karim on corruption charges. The minister left his post, but the result of the corruption investigation by Iraqi Kurdistan Independent Human Rights Commission was not made public.

The Central Bank leads the government's efforts to combat money laundering and terrorist financing. Through the offices of Banking Supervision and Financial Intelligence, the Central Bank worked with law enforcement agencies and the judiciary to identify and prosecute illicit financial transactions. The investigatory capacity of authorities remained extremely limited, although they were successful in prosecuting money-laundering cases linked to financial transfers to Da'esh-controlled territories. The COI, which prosecutes money-laundering cases linked to official corruption, suffered from a lack of investigatory capacity. There also was a lack of political will to prosecute senior officials.

The Council of Ministers Secretariat has an anticorruption advisor, and the COR has an Integrity Committee. The Joint Anti-Corruption Council reporting to the Council of Ministers oversees and monitors compliance with the government's 2010-14 anticorruption strategy. The secretary general for the Council of Ministers led the anticorruption council, which also included the chairperson of the Federal Board of Supreme Audit, the commissioner of the COI, and representatives from the offices of the inspectors general (IGs). When the agenda of the anticorruption council calls for high-level government participation, the Ministry of Interior's head of economic crimes may attend. Despite the council's mandate, the public generally regarded it as having little effect due to the scale of official corruption. The COI's National Strategy to Combat Corruption (2015-19) aims to increase training and development of staff of the IG's office and COI.

Lack of agreement about institutional roles, insufficient political will, political influence, poor transparency, and unclear governing legislation and regulatory processes hampered joint efforts to combat corruption. Although anticorruption institutions increasingly collaborated with civil society groups, organizing workshops, surveys, and training courses, the impact of expanded cooperation was limited. Media and NGOs continued to attempt to expose corruption independently, although their capacity to do so was limited. Anticorruption, law enforcement, and judicial officials, as well as members of civil society and media, faced threats and intimidation in their efforts to combat corrupt practices (see section 2.a.).

Government officials frequently contended that corruption investigations were highly politicized. In December 2015 the COI formed an investigative and oversight committee, consisting of the Iraqi High Judicial Council, the Board of Supreme Audit, and the parliament's integrity committee, and, earlier in the year, added the public prosecutor. The results of the oversight committee's investigations were not made public. The chairman of the COI investigative committee said the COI investigated 630 corruption cases from January through September, resulting in 18 arrest warrants against 18 ministerial-level officials, and 137 arrest warrants for directors general.

On August 11, the UN Development Program and the government signed an agreement to strengthen the capacity of the government to detect, investigate, and prosecute high-profile and complex corruption cases.

In August 2015 the prime minister announced, and the COR approved, a series of reforms designed to eliminate official corruption and to improve public services. The reforms went into effect in 2015, but implementation was inconsistent. Prime Minister Abadi's plan called for the end of sectarian quotas in determining senior positions, as well as the establishment of an executive committee to select ministers, advisors, and directors general based on merit and competence.

The reforms reduced the number of government ministries from 33 to 22. Although the eliminated ministries lost their official mandate, working-level employees continued to be paid while the Council of Ministers engaged in protracted negotiations to merge ministries and reassign employees from eliminated ministries.

Approximately 500 staff members from the Ministry of Human Rights were transferred to the Iraq High Commission for Human Rights, whose Board had not met since May. The reform package authorized a high commission to reopen and investigate old corruption cases. The government subsequently referred 2,000 corruption cases to the courts for prosecution; however, the vast majority of these cases dated from 2003 to 2005.

The prime minister also called on the judiciary to appoint expert judges known for their integrity to investigate and prosecute corruption cases. In 2015 authorities appointed 34 new judges to courts across the country, and 19 integrity judges to Baghdad courts. The Baghdad Integrity Court--an investigation court that specializes in integrity cases--announced it was investigating dozens of corruption cases involving many government ministries. On March 22, the Integrity Court announced it had adjudicated 611 cases; the results of the court decisions were not publicly available. The court in Basrah had not issued any opinions by year's end.

On July 7, the Executive Board of the International Monetary Fund approved a three-year $5.34 billion stand-by arrangement that calls for the government to take measures through June 2019 to combat corruption.

In March media reported on a corruption scandal involving the Ministry of Oil, South Oil Company, and Minister of Higher Education Hussein al-Shahristani. Unaoil, a company based in Monaco, allegedly funneled millions of dollars from U.S. and European clients to government officials as bribes for government contracts. No arrests were made by year's end.

Widespread and pervasive corruption and lack of government transparency, including with regard to oil revenue, were major problems in the IKR. According to the Kurdistan Commission on Public Integrity, corruption in the IKR was extensive. Weak budgetary oversight and lack of training for personnel further hindered the commission from fighting corruption effectively. Allegations and rumors of missing oil revenue were rampant. On October 5, in an effort to improve its capability to deal with corruption, the KRG signed a master service agreement with major international accounting firms to conduct an independent audit of its oil production, marketing, and revenues.

According to local media reports, the KRG made efforts to prosecute corruption cases. On January 24, the IKR presidency confiscated 251 billion dinars ($276 million) from the ex-wife of the KRG minister of natural resources over allegations of corruption. On April 13, the head of the Kurdistan Region's Central Bank and his deputy were arrested on charges of corruption related to an alleged illegal bond-trading scheme. During the year KRG officials at the director general level and below were arrested on corruption charges at the Ministry of Martyrs and Anfal Affairs and Sulaimaniyah Immigration Department.

Financial Disclosure: The law authorizes the COI to obtain annual financial disclosures from senior public officials, including ministers, governors, and parliamentarians, and to take legal action for nondisclosure. Penalties range from fines to imprisonment. A unified system for enforcing annual financial disclosures did not exist. The COI has no jurisdiction over the IKR, but Kurdish members of the central government were required to conform to the law. The law obligates the COI to provide public annual reports on prosecutions, transparency, accountability, and ethics of public service.

The Kurdistan Commission on Public Integrity is responsible for distributing and collecting financial disclosure forms in the IKR. The commission reported that the Kurdistan region's president, all members of its parliament, and all cabinet ministers had submitted financial disclosure reports for 2015. There was no information available indicating that public officials faced penalties for financial nondisclosure.

Public Access to Information: The law does not provide public access to government information. The IKR Information Law expands citizens' rights to request information from the regional government, parliament, and court system, except in cases of national security or classified information. According to the IKR's Human Rights Commission, the government had not implemented this law.

Section 5. Governmental Attitude Regarding International and Nongovernmental Investigation of Alleged Violations of Human Rights

Domestic and international NGOs operated in most cases with little government interference. Due to the humanitarian crisis, the majority of local NGOs shifted their focus to providing assistance to IDPs and other communities the conflict has affected. In some instances these local NGOs worked in coordination with central government and Kurdistan regional government authorities. A number of NGOs also investigated and published findings on human rights cases. When NGOs alleged human rights abuses that concerned government actions or actions of ethnic or religious groups allied with the government, there were some reports of government interference.

NGOs faced capacity-related challenges, did not have regular access to government officials, and did not systematically serve as bulwarks against failures in governance and human rights abuses. Sustainability of domestic NGOs remained a key factor hindering the long-term development of the sector. The government rarely awarded NGOs contracts for services. While the law forbids NGOs from engaging in political activity, political parties or sects originated, funded, or substantially influenced many, although not all, domestic NGOs.

Some NGOs in the South alleged government officials interfered and harassed them, particularly regarding finances. One NGO representative in Dhi Qar said ISF frequently visited the NGO's office, claiming that they needed to "check on things." The governor of Maysan reportedly tried to control funding for local NGOs from international organizations. On September 21, the Maysan Provincial

Council voted to limit the governor's authority over NGOs operating in the province, according to the provincial council's spokesperson, in order to curb the governorate's interruption of local NGOs' work.

Another NGO reported the government refused to register and license its women's shelters. The government periodically asked the NGO to close them down, even though government officials "unofficially" referred women to the shelters. After each such closure, the shelters would reopen a few days later.

The IKR had an active community of mostly Kurdish NGOs, many with close ties and funded by the PUK and KDP political parties. Government funding of NGOs is legally contingent upon whether an NGO's programming goals conform to already-identified priority areas. The region's NGO Directorate established formal procedures for awarding funds to NGOs, which included a public description of the annual budget for NGO funding, priority areas for consideration, deadlines for proposal submission, establishment of a grant committee, and the criteria for ranking proposals. During the year local and international NGOs did not report difficulties registering with the regional government and obtaining permits for their operations in KRG-administered areas.

Reports indicated that Da'esh continued to threaten NGOs and civil society activists in areas under its control throughout the year.

The United Nations or Other International Bodies: The government and the KRG sometimes restricted the access of the United Nations and other international bodies to sensitive locations, including Interior Ministry detention facilities.

Government Human Rights Bodies: In August 2015 the prime minister abolished the Ministry of Human Rights as part of his reform program to reduce the number of governmental ministries. Ministry staff and files were transferred to other ministries, including the Iraqi High Commission for Human Rights (IHCHR), which had not met since May 2015.

The constitution mandates the creation of an independent IHCHR. The law governing its operation provides for commissioners with four-year nonrenewable terms. No less than one-third of the 11 full-time and three reserve commissioners must be women, and at least one full-time member and one reserve member must be from a minority community. The law provides that the IHCHR be financially and administratively independent and have broad authority, including the right to receive and investigate human rights complaints, conduct unannounced visits to correctional facilities, and review legislation. By the end of the year, the commissioners had not been selected.

The KRG Human Rights Commission, which began operating in 2013, issues periodic reports on human rights, trafficking in persons, and religious freedom. The Commission reported KRG police and security organizations had generally been receptive to human rights training and responsive to reports of violations. In February, however, a court convicted the deputy head of the commission's Dahuk office for interfering with a police investigation; his sentence was suspended.

Section 6. Discrimination, Societal Abuses, and Trafficking in Persons

Women

Rape and Domestic Violence: Domestic violence remained a pervasive problem, and there was no law prohibiting domestic violence. The law did not always adequately protect rape victims. The law criminalizes rape (but not spousal rape) and permits a maximum sentence of life imprisonment if the victim dies. The law allows authorities to drop a rape case if the perpetrator marries the victim. There were no reliable estimates of the incidence of rape or information on the effectiveness of government enforcement of the law. Due to social stigma and societal and often familial retribution against both the victim and perpetrator, victims of sexual crimes did not usually report it to authorities or pursue legal remedies. International organizations reported that family-imposed movement restrictions, cultural norms, or stigmatization prohibited or discouraged female victims of sexual crimes from accessing psychosocial support services. Local NGOs in IDP camps in the IKR reported that some Ministry of Health professionals were unwilling to treat sexual assault survivors due to cultural norms, and if they did give care, it was inadequate due to capacity limitations in the health-care sector.

Humanitarian protection experts assessed that conditions in IDP camps were highly conducive to sexual exploitation and abuse, which due to existing social and religious norms, often went unreported.

On September 23, the government signed a joint agreement with UNAMI on the Prevention and Response to Conflict-related Sexual Violence. The government committed to working with the Office of the Special Representative and the UN system to develop and implement an action plan to prevent and respond to conflict-related sexual violence.

Due to continuing Da'esh-perpetrated violence, women's status continued to suffer severe setbacks (see also sections 1.g. and 6). During the year Da'esh continued: to kidnap women and girls; sell, rent, or gift them as forced "brides" (a euphemism for forced marriage or sexual slavery) to Da'esh fighters and commanders; and exploit the promise of sexual access in propaganda materials as part of its recruitment strategy. The Iraq Foundation, a local NGO, reported that Da'esh raped women; victims who refused were beaten until they passed out. According to an August 8 UN Population Fund report, Da'esh continued to sell Yezidi women and girls on slave markets.

In August the Council of Ministers launched the executive plan to implement UN Security Council Resolution 1325, which was passed in 2000 and aimed to increase women's participation in civic life. NGOs reported, however, that government activity to advance it was minimal. In December the government established the Department of Women's Empowerment in the Office of the General Secretary for the Council of Ministers.

There is no law against domestic violence. Local and international NGOs and media reported that domestic violence often went unreported and unpunished, with abuses customarily addressed within the family and tribal structure. Harassment of legal personnel who sought to pursue domestic violence cases under laws criminalizing assault, as well as a lack of trained police and judicial personnel, further hampered efforts to bring perpetrators to justice.

Public policy prevents NGOs from maintaining shelters, which severely limited the number of NGO-run shelters available to victims of gender-based crimes and their ability to access health care and psychosocial support. The Organization for Women's Freedom in Iraq (OWFI) recommended legislation to provide a legal status for women's shelters administered by NGOs. While the government does not have a law that explicitly prohibits NGO-run shelters, current law allows the Ministry of Labor and Social Affairs to determine if a shelter can remain open. OWFI reported that many communities viewed the shelters as brothels and asked the government to close them down. To appease community concerns the ministry regularly closed shelters, only to allow them to reopen in another location and at a later date.

The Ministry of Interior maintained 16 family protection units around the country, which aimed to resolve domestic disputes and establish safe refuges for victims of sexual or gender-based violence. These units tended to prioritize family reconciliation over victim protection and lacked the capacity to support victims. Hotline calls went to the male commanders of the units, which did not follow a regular referral system to provide victims with services, such as legal aid or safe shelter. Victims of domestic violence in Basrah told UNAMI they feared approaching the family protection units, because they suspected that police would immediately inform their families of their testimonies. Shelters for victims of domestic abuse were limited; the family protection units in most locations did not operate shelters. Safe houses, which the government and NGOs operated, were often targets for violence. Minority Rights Group International, an EU-funded human rights organization, noted that the Ministry of Interior Family Protection Units, responsible for receiving complaints about domestic violence, recorded a total of 22,442 cases of family violence across the country between 2010 and November 2014, the latest date for which statistics were available.

The law in the IKR makes domestic violence, including physical and psychological abuse, threats of violence, and spousal rape, a crime. The government implemented the provisions of the law, creating a special police force to investigate cases of gender-based violence and establish a family reconciliation committee within the judicial system, but local NGOs reported that these programs were not effective at combating gender-based violence.

In the IKR, one privately operated shelter and four labor ministry-operated shelters provided some protection and assistance for female victims of gender-based violence and human trafficking. Space was limited, and service delivery was poor. NGOs played a key role in providing services, including legal aid, to victims of domestic violence, who often received no assistance from the government. Instead of using legal remedies, authorities frequently attempted to mediate between women and their families so that the women returned to their homes. Other than marrying or returning to their families, which often resulted in further victimization by the family or community, there were few options for women accommodated at shelters.

According to the KRG Human Rights Commission, there were 7,436 cases of violence against women, 125 cases of self-immolation, 64 suicides, 54 homicides, and 124 cases of rape and sexual abuse reported during the year.

Female Genital Mutilation/Cutting (FGM/C): The Family Violence Law, which went into effect in 2011 in the IKR, bans FGM/C, but NGOs reported the practice persisted, particularly in rural areas. UNAMI reported three women were arrested and charged with FGM/C this year. In coordination with the KRG High Council of

Women Affairs, the KRG Ministry of Planning, and UNICEF, Heartland Alliance International conducted a FGM/C survey of 5,990 mothers of girls four to 14 years of age living in the IKR in 2015 and 2016. Among the mothers surveyed, 44.8 percent reported undergoing FGM/C themselves compared with 10.7 percent of their daughters, with higher rates of FGM/C in Erbil and Sulaimaniyah Governorates. International human rights organization WADI's, and local women's rights organization PANA's, interviews indicated 25 percent of women in the central and southern parts of the country had been subjected to FGM/C.

Other Harmful Traditional Practices: Honor killings remained a serious problem throughout the country, although perpetrators were rarely punished. Some families arranged honor killings to appear as suicides. The law permits honor considerations to mitigate sentences. For example, a provision limits a sentence for murder to a maximum of three years in prison if a man is on trial for killing his wife or a female dependent due to suspicion that the victim was committing adultery.

UNAMI documented several cases of honor killings in Dhi-Qar, Basrah, and Muthanna. On January 16, authorities in Basrah found the body of a 15-year-old girl, reportedly an IDP. She had been decapitated, her head wrapped in a hijab, and thrown into a garbage can.

In March a Basrawi man confessed to the police that he killed his sister because he suspected she was in a sexual relationship. He was released from prison after 24 hours and never went to trial. In August police arrested a man after he stabbed his 20-year-old daughter to death for dating a fellow student at her university in Dhi Qar. He claimed that her death was an accident. At year's end, the case was in court; he was not in prison.

There were multiple reports of women in Basrah and Dhi Qar Governorates committing suicide through self-immolation. Media usually reported these women killed themselves because of family problems.

Women and girls were at times sexually exploited through so-called temporary marriages, a practice more common in Shia than in Sunni traditions, under which a man gives the family of the girl or woman dowry money in exchange for permission to "marry" her for a specified period of time. Government officials and international and local NGOs also reported that the traditional practice of "fasliya" --whereby family members, including women and children, are traded to settle tribal disputes--remained a problem, particularly in southern governorates.

A group called The Committee for the Promotion of Virtue and Prevention of Vice distributed flyers in Maysan Governorate calling for single women to wear the abaya, a full-length, loose robe. Those who refused, according to the flyers, were depraved and unfit for marriage. The flyers also said women should not wear make-up, smile, or laugh with strangers. The Provincial Council held an urgent meeting of the security committee in response to the flyers, but the results of this meeting were not known.

Sexual Harassment: The law prohibits sexual relations outside marriage, including rape or sexual solicitation that may occur during sexual harassment. The penalties include fines and imprisonment. The law provides relief from penalties if unmarried participants marry. No information was available regarding the effectiveness of government enforcement. The labor law that went into effect in February prohibits, for the first time, sexual harassment in the workplace. Due to social conventions and retribution against both the victim and perpetrator of sexual harassment, victims of sexual harassment usually did not pursue legal remedies. Because of the unequal social status of women, their fear of telling close relatives, and their distrust of the criminal justice process, victims rarely filed police complaints against their offenders. In most areas there were few or no publicly provided women's shelters, information, support hotlines, and little or no sensitivity training for police.

UNAMI repeatedly highlighted the need for women's shelters outside the IKR. Women and girls who were victims of sexual harassment or worst forms of abuse were often sent to prison or held in police lock-ups for their own protection in the absence of shelters. Some women, with no alternatives, became homeless.

Reproductive Rights: Couples and individuals have the right to decide the number, timing, and spacing of their children; manage their reproductive health; and have access to the information and means to do so, free from discrimination, coercion, or violence. Due to general insecurity in the country and attendant economic difficulties, many women nonetheless received inadequate medical care. The United Nations reported that sexual and reproductive health services, trauma counselling centers, and reintegration support were severely limited, including in the IKR, where the majority of returned captives lived, often having suffered severe trauma at the hands of Da'esh. There were no reports of women having been denied access to contraception or maternal health services because of a spouse or other family member withholding permission. The Global Justice Center reported in April that Da'esh continued to force captive Yezidi women to have abortions because they viewed sex with a pregnant woman to be forbidden.

<u>Discrimination</u>: Although the constitution forbids discrimination based on gender, conservative societal standards impeded women's ability to enjoy the same legal status and rights as men in all aspects of the judicial system. Throughout the country, women reported increasing social pressure to adhere to conservative social norms. Da'esh continued to impose severe restrictions on women's movement and dress in areas it controlled, and Da'esh patrols were reportedly routine occurrences. The IHCHR reported cases of Da'esh executing women for not wearing the veil.

In March, UNAMI reported that women constituted 51 percent of the country's IDPs. The UN representative for women's affairs in Iraq, Hiba Qaskas, said the abolition of the Ministry for Women's Affairs posed an additional challenge in addressing issues of conflict and displacement, especially since the majority of those displaced were women.

Law and custom generally do not respect freedom of movement for women. For example, the law prevents a woman from applying for a passport without the consent of her male guardian or a legal representative. Women could not obtain the Civil Status Identification Document--required for access to public services, food assistance, health care, employment, education, and housing--without consent of a male relative. This restriction affected women in conflict, according to local NGOs. In Da'esh-controlled areas, Da'esh forces reportedly forbade women from leaving their homes unless male relatives escorted them. Da'esh also prevented professional women from returning to work, with the exception of medical workers and teachers. In August 2015, as part of the prime minister's reform package, authorities dissolved the Ministry of State for Women's Affairs, which had functioned primarily as an advisory office without an independent budget. The former ministry was largely ineffective at solving problems facing women, according to civil society and international women's rights groups. The NGO community called for the government to replace the ministry with another institution. By year's end the government had not indicated how another ministry or institution would cover women's issues or how the institution would be resourced.

Children

<u>Birth Registration</u>: The constitution states that anyone born to at least one citizen parent is a citizen. Failure to register births resulted in the denial of public services such as education, food, and health care. Single women and widows often had problems registering their children. Although in most cases authorities provided birth certificates after registration of the birth through the Ministries of Health and Interior, this was reportedly a lengthy and at times complicated process. The government was generally committed to children's rights and welfare, although it denied benefits to noncitizen children. Families of noncitizen children had to pay for services, such as public schools and health services that were otherwise free.

<u>Education</u>: Primary education is compulsory for citizen children for the first six years of schooling and until the age of 15 in IKR. Equal access to education for girls remained a challenge, particularly in rural and unsecure areas. The net overall completion rate for primary school was 50 percent as of 2013, the latest-year data available. Children in rural areas faced greater education challenges. The IKR primary school completion rate was among the highest in the country, with 65 percent of children completing primary school on time. A lack of available schools, lack of identification documents, limited income with which to purchase required supplies, and a lack of transportation often prevented IDP children from attending schools.

The continuing conflict delayed the academic school year as IDPs throughout the country sheltered in schools. According to a June UNICEF report, 3.5 million school-aged children were unable to access school or any form of education. Nearly one in five schools was not functioning due to the conflict. Since 2014 UNICEF verified 135 attacks on educational facilities and personnel, and 797 schools were taken over as shelters for IDPs.

<u>Child Abuse</u>: Violence against children remained a significant problem. According to a UN-supported study in 2011 (the latest year for available comprehensive figures), 46 percent of girls between the ages of 10 and 14 were exposed to family violence. In 2013 the COR amended the social care law to increase protection for children who were victims of domestic violence. The amendment also called for protection and care of children in shelters, state houses, and orphanages. UNICEF reported in June that over the past 30 months, 1,496 children had been abducted and had been forced into fighting or had been sexually abused.

The KRG's Ministries of Labor and Social Affairs, Education, and Culture and Youth continued to operate a toll-free hotline to report violations against, or seek advice regarding, children's rights.

Early and Forced Marriage: The legal minimum age of marriage is 15 with parental permission and 18 without. The government made few efforts to enforce the law. Traditional forced marriages of girls as young as age 11 continued, particularly in rural areas. According to UNICEF, approximately 975,000 girls in Iraq were married before the age of 15, twice as many as in 1990. Early and forced marriages, as well as abusive temporary marriages, were more prevalent in Da'esh-controlled areas. UNICEF reported that traditional cultural practices and economic hardships also motivated IDP and Syrian refugee families to marry girls at a young age. In December 2015 the KRG Women High Council launched a one-year education and awareness campaign against child marriage in the IKR.

Local and international NGOs reported that forced divorce--the practice of husbands or their families threatening to divorce wives they married when the girls were very young (ages 12 to 16) to pressure the girl's family to provide additional money to the girl's husband and his family--also occurred, particularly in the South. Victims of forced divorce were compelled to leave their husbands and their husbands' families, and social customs regarding family honor often prevented victims from returning to their own families, leaving some adolescent girls abandoned.

Female Genital Mutilation/Cutting (FGM/C): See information in women's section above.

Sexual Exploitation of Children: The law prohibits the commercial exploitation of children, and pornography of any kind, including child pornography. During the year there were multiple reports of Da'esh forces abducting girls and forcing them into marriage with Da'esh fighters (see section 1.g.). Child prostitution was a problem, and anecdotal evidence suggested the problem was particularly serious among Syrian refugees in the IKR. Because the age of legal responsibility was nine years old in the central region and 11 in the IKR, authorities often treated sexually exploited children as criminals instead of as victims. Penalties for the commercial exploitation of children range from fines and imprisonment to the death penalty. No information was available regarding the effectiveness of government enforcement.

<u>Displaced Children</u>: Insecurity and active conflict between government forces and Da'esh caused the displacement of large numbers of children. Due to the conflict in Syria, many children and single mothers from Syria also took refuge in the IKR (see section 2.d.).

<u>International Child Abductions</u>: The country is not a party to the 1980 Hague Convention on the Civil Aspects of International Child Abduction. See the Department of State's *Annual Report on International Parental Child Abduction* at travel.state.gov/content/childabduction/en/legal/compliance.html.

Anti-Semitism

A small number of Jewish citizens (estimated at less than 100) lived in Baghdad, and there were unconfirmed reports that small Jewish communities existed in other parts of the country. There were no reports of anti-Semitic acts. In 2015 the KRG Ministry of Endowments and Religious Affairs opened a representative office for Kurdish Jews, which held the IKR's first Holocaust Remembrance Day on May 10. According to unofficial statistics, there were 430 Jewish families in the IKR.

Trafficking in Persons

See the Department of State's *Trafficking in Persons Report* at www.state.gov/j/tip/rls/tiprpt/.

Persons with Disabilities

Although the constitution states the government, through law and regulations, should care for and rehabilitate persons with disabilities in order to reintegrate them into society, there are no laws prohibiting discrimination against persons with physical, sensory, intellectual, or mental disabilities in employment, education, air travel and other transportation, access to health care, the judicial system, or the provision of other state services. There were reports that persons with disabilities continued to experience discrimination due to social stigma. Although the Council of Ministers issued a decree ordering access for persons with disabilities to buildings and to educational and work settings, incomplete implementation limited access. Local NGOs reported many children with disabilities dropped out of public school due to insufficient physical access to school buildings, a lack of appropriate learning materials in schools, and a shortage of teachers qualified to work with children with developmental or intellectual disabilities. NGOs also reported that authorities denied some children with physical disabilities access to schools.

The minister of labor and social affairs leads a commission for persons with disabilities, designed to remain independent of the government. The KRG deputy minister of labor and social affairs leads a similar commission, administered by a special director within the ministry.

There is a 5 percent public-sector employment quota for persons with disabilities, but employment discrimination persisted, and observers projected that the quota was not likely met at year's end (see also section 7.d.). Government and KRG officials reported they had few resources to accommodate persons with disabilities in prisons, detention centers, and temporary holding facilities. Mental health support for prisoners with mental disabilities did not exist.

The Ministry of Health provided medical care, benefits, and rehabilitation, when available, for persons with disabilities, who could also receive benefits from other agencies, including the Prime Minister's Office. The Ministry of Labor and Social Affairs operated several institutions for children and young adults with disabilities. The ministry maintained loans programs for persons with disabilities for vocational training.

National/Racial/Ethnic Minorities

The country's population included Arabs, Kurds, Turkmen, and Shabaks as well as ethnic and religious minorities, including Chaldeans, Assyrians, Armenian Orthodox, Syriacs, Yezidis, Sabean-Mandean, Bahai, Kaka'i, and a very small number of Jews. The country also had a small Romani community, as well as an estimated 500,000 citizens of African descent, referred to as "Black Iraqis," who reside primarily in Basrah and the South. In April 2015 the Ministry of Religion in the IKR officially registered a variant of Zoroastrianism, locally known as Zaradashti, as a religion.

In October 2015 parliament passed The National Identity Card Law, which came into effect in February. This law automatically registers minor children as Muslims if they are born to at least one Muslim parent, or if either parent converts from another religion to Islam. Additionally, the law does not allow non-Muslims to self-identify with their ethnic group nor does it allow Muslims to convert to other religions.

In areas under its control, Da'esh committed numerous abuses against Yezidis, Shabaks, Christians, and other minority communities, including execution, kidnapping, rape, enslavement, forced marriage, forced abortions, expulsion, theft, forced conversions, and destruction of property. Activists from religious and ethnic minority communities faced the greatest risk. Other illegal armed groups also targeted ethnic and religious minority communities (see section 1.g.).

Many of the estimated 500,000 persons of African descent lived in extreme poverty with high rates of illiteracy and unemployment. "Black Iraqis" were not represented in politics and did not hold any high-level government positions.

There were reports of KRG authorities discriminating against minorities, including Turkmen, Arabs, Yezidis, Shabaks, and Christians, both in the disputed territories and in the three provinces that officially make up the Kurdistan region.

Although Arabs are the majority in most of the country, they are a minority in Kirkuk, and Arab residents of the city frequently charged that KRG security forces targeted Arab communities. Arab residents of Kirkuk alleged that local authorities used the pretext of terrorist attacks to impose curfews on them and arrest Arabs who lacked legal resident permits.

Kirkuk citizens, particularly members of the Sunni Arab community, faced pressure to return to their areas of origin. UNAMI received reports of evictions, confiscation of identity documents, or notifications to leave Kirkuk throughout the year. NGOs reported Kirkuk authorities confiscated identification documents of IDPs from Salah al-Din, Anbar, and Diyala Governorates. As of September local authorities notified approximately 6,000 families in Laylan Camp and in a dozen neighborhoods in Kirkuk that they had to return to their areas of origin (see section 2.d.). When confronted by international organizations and the diplomatic community about forced expulsions of IDPs, Kirkuk authorities denied issuing such an order. International organizations and NGOs continued to assert that the government was indirectly pressuring IDPs to leave.

Acts of Violence, Discrimination, and Other Abuses Based on Sexual Orientation and Gender Identity

Neither hate crime nor antidiscrimination laws exist, and there are no other criminal justice mechanisms to aid in the prosecution of crimes motivated by bias against members of the LGBTI community. Despite repeated threats and violence targeting LGBTI individuals, the government failed to identify, arrest, or prosecute attackers or to protect targeted individuals.

No law specifically prohibits consensual same-sex sexual activity, although the law prohibits sodomy, irrespective of gender. There was no data on prosecutions for sodomy.

Authorities relied on public indecency charges or confessions of monetary exchange (that is for prostitution, which is illegal) to prosecute same-sex sexual activity. Authorities used the same charges to arrest heterosexual persons involved in sexual relations with persons other than their spouses.

The law does not address discrimination based on sexual orientation or gender identity. Societal discrimination in employment, occupation, and housing based on sexual orientation, gender identity, and unconventional appearance was common. Information was not available regarding discrimination in access to education or health care.

Due to stigma, intimidation, and potential harm including violent attacks, LGBTI organizations did not operate openly, nor were there gay pride marches or gay rights advocacy events. LGBTI persons often faced abuse and violence from family and nongovernmental actors. In addition to targeted violence, members of the LGBTI community remained at risk for honor crimes, since their conduct did not conform to traditional gender norms. LGBTI rights groups attributed the lack of publicized cases of attacks to the low profile of members of the LGBTI community, who altered their public dress and lifestyle to conform to societal norms. NGOs established shelters for individuals who feared attacks and continued to accommodate victims. They periodically received threats and relocated shelters for security reasons. Community activists reported that violence and intimidation continued.

In July, Shia cleric Muqtada al-Sadr publicly stated that homosexuals should not be attacked as they suffered from psychological problems.

Da'esh published videos depicting alleged executions of persons accused of homosexual activity that included stoning and being thrown from buildings. In July, UNAMI reported a young man had been abducted and killed in Baghdad because of his sexual orientation. Sources reported the abductors were known members of armed groups. Some armed groups also started a campaign against homosexual persons in Baghdad, UNAMI reported at least three more LGBTI persons had disappeared since July.

Other Societal Violence or Discrimination

In July religious leaders, members of parliament, and Baghdad-based judges said some political parties sanctioned criminal networks seizing Christian property. Christian groups also reported they had submitted dozens of complaints to the parliamentary integrity committee, and in August had sent a letter, signed by Assyrian Member of Parliament Yunadim Kanna, to the prime minister outlining cases of illegal seizure of Christians' real estate in Baghdad. According to Masarat, a domestic minority rights NGO, most Christians refused to file complaints due to fear that armed groups might abduct their families. Those who filed complaints reported police did not conduct thorough investigations.

Section 7. Worker Rights

a. Freedom of Association and the Right to Collective Bargaining

The constitution states that citizens have the right to form and join unions and professional associations. The law does not prohibit antiunion discrimination or provide reinstatement for workers fired for union activity. In August 2015 the COR approved a labor law (No. 37 of 2015) that allows workers to select representatives for collective bargaining, even if they are not members of a union, and affords workers the right to have more than one union in a workplace. The law went into effect in February 7. On October 25, the Council of Ministers ratified International Labor Organization Convention 87 on freedom of association and the rights to organize, but the COR had not voted on it at year's end.

A Saddam Hussein-era law bans all public-sector trade union activity. The law also considers individuals state-owned enterprises employ (who made up approximately 10 percent of the workforce) as public-sector employees. Civil society organizations lobbied for a new trade union law to expand union rights.

Private-sector employees in worksites employing more than 50 workers may form workers committees--subdivisions of unions with limited rights--but most private-sector businesses employed fewer than 50 workers.

Labor courts have the authority to consider alleged labor law violations and disputes, but no information was available concerning enforcement of the applicable law, including whether procedures were prompt or efficient.

Strikers and union leaders reported that government officials threatened and harassed them during the year. They also asserted that ministries and state-owned enterprises used fines, demotions, suspension from work, and forced transfers to punish labor activists and discourage union activity. Unions reported authorities arrested labor leaders and activists for their activities. Union leaders also cited corruption within the government as a continuous problem, with government officials imposing arbitrary fines on workers for such activities as calling for demonstrations and traveling outside the country on union business without prior approval.

The law allows for collective bargaining in the private sector, although in practice, the government authorities sometimes violated private-sector employees' collective bargaining rights. Some unions were able to play a supportive role in labor disputes, and they had the right to demand government arbitration.

b. Prohibition of Forced or Compulsory Labor

The law prohibits all forms of forced or compulsory labor--including slavery, indebtedness, and trafficking in persons--but the government did not effectively monitor or enforce the law.

Foreign migrant workers, particularly construction workers, security guards, cleaners, handymen, and domestic workers, were subjected to forced labor, confiscation of travel and identity documents, restrictions on movement and communications, physical abuse, sexual harassment and rape, withholding of wages, and forced overtime. There were cases of employers withholding travel documents, stopping payment on contracts, and preventing foreign employees from leaving the work site.

Women were subjected to involuntary domestic service through forced marriages and the threat of divorce, and women who fled such marriages or whose husbands divorced them were vulnerable to further forced labor. Due to the deterioration in the security situation, female IDPs were increasingly vulnerable to economic exploitation and discriminatory employment conditions. According to local sources, Da'esh exploited as many as several thousand Yezidi and other minority women and girls sexually and economically and forced men and boys into military service (see also sections 1.g. and 6).

Also, see the Department of State's *Trafficking in Persons Report* at www.state.gov/j/tip/rls/tiprpt/.

c. Prohibition of Child Labor and Minimum Age for Employment

The constitution and law prohibit child labor. The minimum age for employment is 15. The law limits working hours for persons younger than age 18 to seven hours a day and prohibits employment in work detrimental to health, safety, or morals of anyone younger than 18. The labor code does not apply to juveniles (ages 15 to 18) who work in family-owned businesses producing goods exclusively for domestic use. Since children employed in family enterprises are exempt from some protections in the labor code with regard to employment conditions, anecdotal reports of children performing hazardous work in family-owned businesses, such as in brick manufacturing and auto repair shops, continued. The new labor law introduced improvements to child labor regulations, such as increased fines and penalties for violators of the labor law. The new law abolished a Saddam-era decree that allowed children as young as 12 to work. The law also mandates employers--not workers or families--to bear the cost of annual medical checks for working juveniles (ages 15-18). Children between the ages of 12 and 14 were not required to attend school but were not permitted to work and thus were vulnerable to the worst forms of child labor. Violators are subject to imprisonment for a period of 30 days to six months or to a fine ranging from 100,000 dinars to 500,000 dinars ($91 to $455). Qualitative data on child labor practices was limited, particularly with regard to the worst forms of child labor, a factor that further limited enforcement of existing legal protections.

Child labor, including in its worst forms, occurred throughout the country. The inspection service of the labor ministry sought to comply with the law prohibiting child labor in the private and public sectors. Inspections continued, but due to capacity constraints as well as the focus on maintaining security and fighting terrorism, law enforcement personnel and labor inspectors' efforts to monitor these practices were ineffective, and penalties for violations did not serve as a deterrent.

The NGO Iraqi Observatory for Human Rights documented many cases of displaced children who were forced to migrate with their families from their homes, and were subsequently forced to work. It also reported the Ministry of Labor and Social Affairs did not maintain accurate statistics about displaced child workers. In July, UNICEF reported an estimated half a million children were in the labor market, a number which doubled since 1990.

There was no recent survey of the child labor situation in the IKR, but local NGOs reported that child labor increased due to the influx of Syrian refugees. The IKR's Labor Ministry operated a 24-hour hotline for reporting labor abuses, including child labor; the hotline received approximately 200 calls per month.

There were reports that Da'esh and other armed groups recruited children to gather intelligence, staff checkpoints, patrol the streets, and serve as couriers (see section 1.g. and section 6, Children). There was no evidence that the government purposely recruited children into the armed forces. There were local press reports of families sending their children to beg in the streets. Local NGOs reported that organized gangs also recruited children to beg. In September the Labor Ministry launched a grants program to encourage low-income families to send their children to school rather than to beg in the streets.

See also the Department of Labor's *Findings on the Worst Forms of Child Labor* at www.dol.gov/ilab/reports/child-labor/findings.

d. Discrimination with Respect to Employment and Occupation

The constitution provides that all citizens are equal before the law without regard to gender, sect, opinion, belief, nationality, or origin. The law prohibits discrimination based on race, sex, religion, social origin, political opinion, language, or social status, and any forms of sexual harassment in the workplace. The government was ineffective in enforcing these provisions. The law does not prohibit discrimination based on disability, age, sexual orientation or gender identity, HIV-positive status or other communicable diseases.

Discrimination in employment and occupation occurred with respect to women, foreign workers, and minorities (see section 6). The law gives migrant Arab workers the same status as citizens but does not provide the same rights for non-Arab migrant workers, who faced stricter residency and work visa requirements.

e. Acceptable Conditions of Work

In June the prime minister issued an order to cut senior civil servants salaries by 15 percent due to budget constraints. The COR rejected the order in July. The 2015 pay scale reduced salaries of senior civil servants and increased salaries of civil servants at the low end of the pay scale. The 2015 pay scale offered nonskilled workers a monthly salary of 170,000 dinars ($155) and 300,000 dinars ($273) for jobs that required a bachelor's degree. The salary also included bonuses for employees with families and higher education degrees.

The law limits the standard workday to eight hours, with one or more rest periods totaling 30 minutes to one hour, and the standard workweek to 48 hours. The law permits up to four hours of overtime work per day and requires premium pay for overtime work. For industrial work, overtime should not exceed one hour per day. The government sets occupational health and safety standards. The law states that for hazardous or exhausting work, employers should reduce daily working hours. The law provides workers the right to remove themselves from a situation endangering health and safety without prejudice to their employment but does not extend this right to civil servants or migrant workers, who together made up the majority of the country's workforce.

The Labor Ministry has jurisdiction over labor law, child labor, wages, occupational safety and health topics, and labor relations. The government did not enforce regulations governing working conditions. The ministry's occupational safety and health staff worked throughout the country, but the lack of a law governing these inspections hindered compliance and enforcement efforts.

The legal and regulatory framework, combined with the country's high level of violence and insecurity, high unemployment, large informal sector, and lack of meaningful work standards, resulted in unacceptable conditions for many workers. Workplace injuries occurred frequently, especially among manual laborers. A lack of oversight and monitoring of employment contracts left foreign and migrant workers vulnerable to exploitative working conditions and abusive treatment. Little information was available on the total number of foreign workers in the country, although some observers reported that large groups of migrant workers, many of them in the country illegally, lived in work camps, sometimes in substandard conditions. Due to the deterioration in security, and conflict throughout western and northern Iraq, many foreign workers departed the country, or their companies or home governments evacuated them. The government also deported dozens of foreign workers from the South because they lacked proper immigration documents.

On February 5, a fire in an Erbil hotel massage center resulted in at least 19 deaths. Press reports quoted the Erbil governor as identifying 15 of the victims as

Philippine nationals; the remaining victims were Iraqi and Palestinian. The hotel reportedly lacked fire extinguishers and fire suppression systems.

In 2015 the Labor Ministry launched an income-generating loan program, with a budget of 10 billion dinars ($9.1 million), to assist unemployed persons, including recent college graduates, shopkeepers affected by terrorism, and IDPs. In February the ministry announced that the microloans had benefitted 43,079 persons since the start of the program.

www.ingramcontent.com/pod-product-compliance
Lightning Source LLC
Chambersburg PA
CBHW080903260726
48660CB00009B/3420